ALL YOU NEED TO KNOW™ ABOUT BEING A TRAINEE SOLICITOR

Elizabeth Cruickshank
and
Penny Cooper

LONGTAIL

First published November 2008 by Longtail Limited.
Tel: 020 7938 1975 Fax: 020 7938 3861 Email: info@longtail.eu
Web: www.allyouneedtoknowguides.com

Publisher and Editor-in-chief:	James Piesse
Deputy Editor:	Sheenagh Nixon
Assistant Publisher:	Kirra Smeaton
Editorial Assistant:	Julia Gibson
Sub-editor:	Monica Kendall
Typesetting:	Louise Downer
Art Director and Illustrator:	Andrew Debens

ISBN: 978-0-9552186-7-5
Printed and bound in Great Britain by Clays Limited

ALL YOU NEED TO KNOW ABOUT BEING A TRAINEE SOLICITOR

ALL YOU NEED TO KNOW ABOUT BEING A TRAINEE SOLICITOR

CONTENTS

circulating – networking rules – after the event.

12. A SPORTING CHANCE

Sporting sociology – golf – choosing players – firm forensics – other sports – team sports – all your leisure?

13. ORGANISATION AND COMMUNICATION

The importance of diaries – calendar management – phone calls – receiving phone calls – deferring communication – listening and writing – telephone rage – patience works – personal calls – unequal status – emails – easy-to-make email errors.

14. YOUR PLACE IN THE OFFICE

Do you deserve your salary? – the cost of mistakes – don't hide mistakes – how to own up – burying bad news – sort it out – sharing a room – getting onside – dealing with unhappiness – getting work.

15. KEEPING HEALTHY

Hard-work city – trainees with a disability – exercise – food – entertaining lunches – social drinking – reality check – drinking buddies – the material alternative.

16. FINANCES

The financial picture – student loan repayments – pensions – getting information – regular savings – taking advice – ISAs – credit cards and store cards – credit cards – office expenses – housing.

17. PROTECTION AND SURVIVAL

Client confidentiality – your belongings – don't be dishonest – harassment and bullying – limitations of understanding – pressure points – analysis – sexual harassment – if it happens, what are your options? – litigation – some hard questions – removing yourself from the situation – sharpen your antennae – going to HR.

18. APPRAISAL INTERVIEWS

Being appraised – presenting your case – talk it up! – how to deal with your failings – making suggestions – how can you improve your supervisor's life? – the year ahead – what can your firm do for you? – appraisal skills – turning negative into positive – under-promise but over-

PREFACE

If you want to get ahead as a trainee solicitor, you need to read this book. Right now you might well be thinking 'not more reading'. You will already have spent many years of your life in study just to get to the point where you could even consider a career in the law. But this book is different from any other book on legal education. Read it and learn the lessons about life in law firms – trust us, it is a worthwhile investment. The time you spend reading this book could save you heaps of worry and days of barking up the wrong tree; it might even save your career.

WHAT THIS BOOK IS ABOUT

If you want to become a successful trainee solicitor – one who gets the training contract in the optimum firm, one whose work is of a high standard and is regarded by partners as an asset to the firm – you need to say and do certain things, which you will not be taught at law school.

Law school education is focused on legal practice, procedure, cases and statutes; on top of all the academic knowledge you will be given, there simply isn't time to teach you one of the most useful skills of all – how to fit into the culture of a law firm. In essence that is the subject of this book.

What exactly is 'the culture of a law firm'? It is simply how things are done in law firms. Of course every firm is different, but there are certain things that are common to the way all law firms operate. The sooner you understand these cultural basics, the easier you will find it to make a success of your career.

Together we have worked for a combined total of about 40 years in and around the legal profession. We knew that there were lessons that we had learned about how lawyers and law firms work and could have learned a lot sooner had someone had the time to show us. Unfortunately most lawyers are incredibly busy working for their clients and don't have much (if any) time to stop and give detailed guidance to young lawyers.

Many of them have barely enough time to coach trainees on law, let alone coach them on how to get ahead or how to feel comfortable in their firms.

We spoke to training and graduate recruitment managers and asked them what they wished trainees knew when they started in law firms; we asked partners what skills, knowledge and attributes they wanted to see in the best trainees. When we showed our book to newly qualified solicitors they told us, without fail, how useful it would have been if they had read it before they started their training contracts.

WHAT IS IN THIS BOOK

This book contains what some would call common sense. But we all know that common sense is not at all common and sometimes things only make sense after you have learned them the hard way. In effect this book contains the combined common sense of a great many people on:

- Handling with ease the legal tasks that are set for you
- Forming excellent relationships with all the people who can help you within the firm (and most importantly how to make it more likely that they will want to help you)
- Preparing effectively for interviews and appraisals
- Looking after yourself, your finances and your career
- Winning over clients and key people in your firm
- Coping with stress and the long hours culture
- Even love and romance should it come your way!

WHAT THIS BOOK IS NOT ABOUT

We assume that law school will teach you what a trainee needs to know about the law (or at least you will know how to find the information).

Although we may tell you cautionary tales about lawyers who earn lots but still don't have enough, we don't pretend to give you financial advice – for financial advice you need to see an independent financial adviser. We don't give you medical or legal advice, although we do point you in the direction of specialists should you need help with addictions or harassment. We don't claim to be specialists in any of these things; if we specialise in anything, it is in putting together the experiences and good advice of trainers and other professionals on how trainees can best progress in their law firms.

It doesn't have to take you years to work out the culture of a law firm. With this book you can avoid some common pitfalls so that you can spend your time concentrating on the job rather than sweating about the other stuff. The other stuff is what we have put in this book; if you can get to grips with it quickly, the chances are (though we can't guarantee it – and you would expect us to say that, wouldn't you, because we're lawyers) that you will have a far better time in your firm and your partners could consider you a star trainee. Which of course you can be, if you make sense of how the law firm works and go about your work accordingly.

WHERE YOU GO FROM HERE

The 'law firm village' and the paths through it can at times seem very confusing and it can be all too easy to lose your way. Think of this book as a routemap which can help you to find a sensible and realistic path through your village to qualification and to a fulfilling and happy career.

Simply reading a routemap is not enough. You have to keep your eyes and ears open and take in your surroundings. Good lawyers are always learning: about the law, about their clients and about each other. So keep asking questions, keep watching and listening and keep reading. Read the trade press (the *Gazette*, *The Lawyer*, the *Solicitors Journal, Legal Week, Legal Business* and magazines which concentrate on your area of law) and the trade websites such as lawsociety.org.uk, totallylegal.com, timesonline.co.uk and telegraph.co.uk.

Take an interest in the latest legislation in your preferred area of law and, just as importantly, take an interest in the latest developments that affect your clients. Learn to understand and assist them – without them there would be no job for you. Now is the time to demonstrate to your firm that you can develop the people skills necessary to gain and keep clients.

Be alert to any potential storms on the horizon for your village. To ensure that you have some notion of the pressures of partnership and law firm management you should also make sure that you are aware of changes that affect the management and regulation of law firms.

Keep asking yourself how you could improve. Stand back and you will realise that having read this book, you now have a better idea of who can help you and what to ask.

Good luck in the village – we wish you an exciting and enjoyable sojourn there.
Elizabeth and Penny

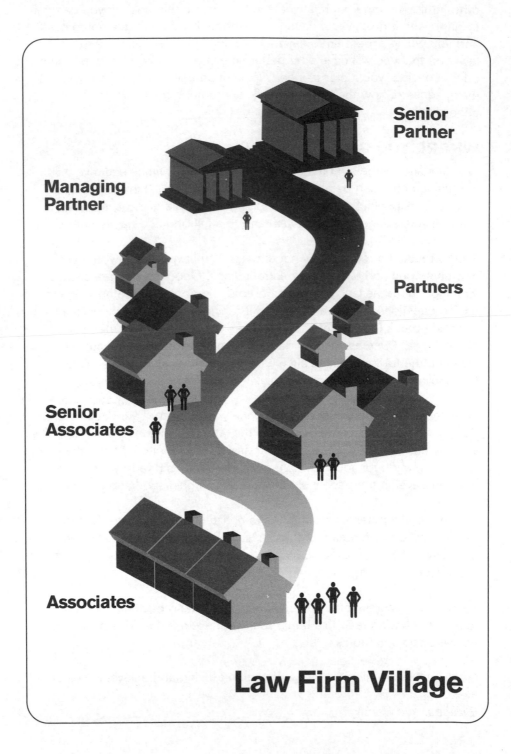

INTRODUCTION

Law firms are villages. Some are hamlets and some seem as large as small towns with distant suburbs, but they all have the village mentality. Villagers are all intensely interested in the goings on of other villagers: how much they earn, their promotion prospects and their relationships – particularly their flirtatious ones. Villages are hotbeds of gossip and law firms are no different. Villages have histories, usually retained and frequently embroidered in the minds of the oldest inhabitants, and law firms are the same. Villagers bear grudges against other villagers, some of which involve other villages, and lawyers are the same.

In passing the time of day in a village you can often pick up useful information and you can do the same in a law firm. But remember that in a village and in a law firm anything that you say and do can be relayed to other people very quickly. Law firms have the added spice that they are connected by other networks so that things that you say and do, if of interest, may rapidly become the common currency of other firms way beyond the boundaries of your own.

Some years ago one married solicitor was conducting an affair with one of the secretaries in his firm. She sent him a salacious email, he thought that he was deleting it, but instead pressed the print button, and by the time he realised what he had done the email had been printed out at the printer outside his office, been picked up by one of the other secretaries, become the subject of gossip and was subsequently reported in the legal press.

One of the very overused words in this book will be the word 'remember'. This is not just because you need to remember things but because other people remember them as well. So, remember that the memory of the funny, incompetent, rude, negligent, arrogant and silly things that you do is likely to live on in the corporate folk memory much longer than the recollection of the clever ones. But if you do make mistakes, remember that other people make them as well.

Chapter 1

CHOOSING A TRAINING FIRM

SPEED READ SUMMARY

- A training contract is a two-party agreement. You need to fit the firm's requirements and the firm should offer you an environment in which you can learn comfortably.

- Before you submit any applications spend time researching the marketplace by looking at websites and brochures, going to recruitment fairs and asking around.

- Be clear about what you want from your training firm. Firms offer benefits other than salary.

- Research yourself as well as the firms. List your strengths and weaknesses and ask someone you trust to do the same. Educational qualifications, work experience and character traits should all be included in this assessment.

- Ask yourself what you can do without and what you can't compromise on in order to get a contract.

- When you have decided on the firms to apply to, spend time on producing persuasive and accurate applications.

IN THE PAST

Once upon a time there were only a few thousand qualified lawyers in the country, law firm villages were very small and trainees (or articled clerks as they were then called) were required to pay for their training. The process of obtaining a training place was very different. Not so long ago, both the following approaches were successful:

■ My father took me along to have lunch with the Senior Partner of the two firms he gave business to and they both offered me articles on the spot.

■ I wrote a short letter to the Senior Partner and told him that I was available to start my articles the following September.

COMPATIBILITY

Now trainees are paid during their training, competition is fiercer and the recruitment process is more complex. The profession is much more diverse and firms look for trainees who will be able to fit in with their colleagues and clients as quickly as possible.

The firm must suit you but you must also suit the firm. They will be investing a great deal of time and money, so they want to recruit trainees who will fit in quickly and who are likely to remain with them for the long haul. You will expect the firms to which you apply to assess you, and you can save a great deal of time and effort by assessing yourself first. Why apply to a City law firm if you really want to practise Legal Aid in Cumbria? Why apply to a firm with a strong competition law bias with an office in Brussels, if you have no capacity for learning languages and are more interested in property law?

Think carefully before you apply to firms that are not an obvious fit for you. Don't feel that you have to apply to particular firms just because your friends are doing so. Don't apply to a firm simply for 'prestige' reasons if there is no other real attraction.

Spending time on research will pay dividends by focusing your thoughts and will save you time in the long run when you are completing your applications. Internet searches can be very revealing in terms of how firms see themselves. Reality may differ, but you do at least get some idea of what they are aiming for. Don't just look at their graduate recruitment pages. Firms design their websites primarily to attract or to provide information for clients and the general public. You can glean some idea of the relative balance of a firm's specialist departments by looking at the amount of space that each department occupies. Some firms also list their clients and recent deals and transactions.

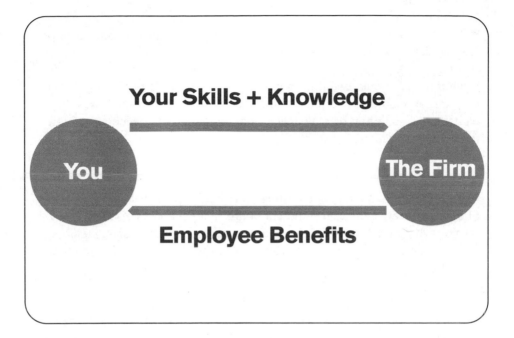

COMPATIBILITY

You should choose a pool of prospective law firms by:
- Analysing what they want and then asking yourself if you fit their criteria
- Asking yourself what you want and then assessing which law firms fit your criteria

SOME INFORMATION SOURCES

The Law Society's Training Contract Handbook

This lists details of over 1,000 firms which offer training contracts. Its sister website LawCareers.net also contains useful information about insights into what law firms are looking for.

The Law Society's website

Although this is not the most user-attractive website, it can render up a surprising amount of useful information. The Find a Solicitor section will enable you to search for particular firms or for firms in particular locations or with particular specialisms. For each firm it will indicate:

- The firm's address, telephone number and website address
- All areas of law covered, languages spoken and whether the firm offers Legal Aid
- Whether the firm is an authorised trainer
- The names of all solicitors in the firm, their year of qualification, area of expertise and languages spoken

From this you should begin to form an idea of the firm's profile. This may be a better source of information about smaller firms than their own websites, which often display only a brief indication of services provided to clients.

Firm websites

Many firms dedicate sections of their websites to potential trainees. Some of these are very informative and some are quite simply opaque. Some will tell you what they are looking for in a trainee and what benefits, including salary, are on offer but in others you will have to deduce this for yourself from the purple prose of their past trainees.

Doing a general Google search on the firm's name may provide further information about their diversity policies, recent deals, the focus of their work and if they have for example merged or are considering merging with another firm. This latter point is important because if individual partners are jockeying for position in a new enlarged firm, they will have less time to be concerned about you. Searching on the names of individual partners may produce silence or may produce information about their interests and list articles that they have written.

Brochures

Not all firms who take on trainees have glossy trainee brochures. Smaller firms are much more likely to focus their marketing efforts on clients. Reading any specialist handouts prepared for clients and/or noting whether they write for or are reported on in the local paper may give you some idea of the main areas of practice of smaller firms.

The legal press

The Lawyer and *Legal Week* both have websites which you can use to search for information on the firm or individual partners. See thelawyer.com and legalweek.com.

Word of mouth

Ask as many people as you can find about firms in which you are interested, whether they are trainees themselves, solicitors or partners, or simply people who have had experience of dealing with them. Your careers adviser may also prove a useful sounding board.

Recruitment fairs and law fairs

Many of the large firms attend and have a stand where you can pick up brochures and ask questions. Many of the solicitors manning the stands are relatively newly qualified themselves. Asking them why they chose their own particular firm can give you invaluable information about that firm. If they say very positive things, then make a note of their names as you might be able to refer to them later during interviews. But if you intend to do that, then remember to check through the Law Society website to make sure that they are still practising with the firm.

Use your eyes

If you can, take a look at a firm's premises. Does it look organised? Toys in the waiting room? They expect family matters. *Country Life*? Agricultural tenancies, trusts and estate planning. Even a glance through the window can give you some idea of a firm's organisation and resources. Although a word of caution here. Some firms have orderly client faces and bedlam behind the scenes, and some partners operate an everything on the top of the desk filing system but have exceptionally ordered minds.

RollonFriday.com

This website is produced by a group of former City lawyers. It provides up-to-date salary information and lists the number of target hours for 52 City firms and rather less information for a small number of other firms in Birmingham, Bristol, Leeds, Manchester and Newcastle. It is also notable for its discussion forums and sometimes irreverent Friday Newsletter, from which you can pick up the odd bit of useful advice.

ALTERNATIVES TO PRIVATE PRACTICE TRAINING CONTRACTS

Most solicitors qualify through having spent the two years of their training contracts with a private practice firm. However, there are alternatives, which although they may not pay as well may be a better fit for your particular personality and circumstances. Local authorities can be particularly attractive if you need to work more certain hours, have longer holidays or work flexitime. They offer a varied work experience covering most business-related legal areas, property and planning law, employment law, education, child protection but not law related to private client affairs.

A few companies do take trainees in their legal departments. Again these will offer experience in company and commercial matters, property and planning law, employment law with pensions and tax-related issues thrown in for good measure. The basic mindset here will be different in that in-house legal advisers not only carry out some of the legal work themselves, but they must be alert as to when to take advice from external law firms. In that case they are the clients and not the adviser. In some ways a working day may be more varied, you will learn more about how business works, but you may also find that your experience has been unduly tied to a particular product or industry.

The Government Legal Service (GLS) takes a few trainees. This is a very competitive option as the GLS recruits most of its solicitors and barristers post-qualification.

MAKING A LIST

Be positive and focus on what you want from your legal training and subsequent career. Make a list of your ideal firm requirements, what you want and what you don't want and where you might be willing to compromise.

Salary

Trainee salaries vary from the current minimum of less than £17,000 to around £40,000, but they can be even higher, particularly in American firms based in London. The level of salary may be important to you for different reasons. You probably owe the student loan company, your bank or your parents a substantial sum for your education so far. You simply 'know' that you will be happier if you earn a high salary. You may feel that salary is an indicator of your personal worth and that the more you earn, the better you will feel about yourself. On the other hand, money may not be an important criterion for you, and it therefore may be the first compromise you are prepared to make when choosing your training firm.

Making a difference

This phrase covers a broad range of possibilities. Legal Aid work may seem the obvious choice here, but may not be possible immediately because trainee salaries at Legal Aid firms are often too small to help you

What are the most important things you are looking for?

- High salary
- Flexible working (flexitime, working from home, holidays in exchange for pay)
- Part-time working (compressed hours, job share, term time/holiday hours)
- Short commute
- Foreign travel
- Being part of a team
- Intellectually stimulating work
- Secondments to other organisations e.g. international clients

What else would you like your employer to provide?

- Pension contributions
- Gym
- Opportunity to do pro bono or charitable work
- Healthcare plan
- Onsite day care
- Commitment to professional development and training
- Clear career prospects and promotion path

much with overhanging student debt. Bear in mind that you may be able to obtain a grant from the Legal Services Commission to help you through training at a Legal Aid firm.

Think beyond Legal Aid. Working in the public sector, for a charity or for a socially responsible not for profit business can also provide a similar sense of 'making a difference'.

There are other ways to 'give back'. Many firms, large and small, have well-structured pro bono activities where their trainees can contribute to the local community while learning about areas of law outside their everyday work. Some firms also benefit their local community by encouraging their trainees to act as mentors to disadvantaged young people.

Flexible working and part-time working

Some, but not many, firms offer the opportunity to undertake the training contract on a part-time basis. Try to find out about this before your interview, as a straight question at interview may be seen as a lack of commitment to the firm. For most trainees flexible working and part-time working are probably not of great importance when they begin their contracts but they could be in the future.

The internet is probably the most discreet information source if you want to find out more about a firm's attitude to flexible working. Website searches using keywords such as 'part-time' or 'flexible' or 'family friendly' in conjunction with the name of a firm you are interested in can yield a surprising amount of information. A large number of female partners in a firm suggests a certain amount of flexibility in working practices, particularly if they mention their children in their individual profiles.

Some firms state positively that their employees can work flexibly or that they have part-time employees. If a firm is often quoted with regard to flexible working, then it is likely that it is at least considering making it available to staff if it has not already done so.

Remember that some areas of law are by their nature potentially less flexible than others. Anything concerned with large corporate transactions or litigation is likely to be less flexible; however, solicitors working in areas of law which are advice-driven rather than negotiation-driven, such as tax and pensions, often find it easier to make flexible arrangements. Working in a small firm is no guarantee that you will be able to work part-time or flexibly in the future; if there are deadlines they still have to be met.

Geographical location

If it is essential that you work in a particular part of the country because you want to be near your family or to pursue particular hobbies, sports or special interests, be aware that insisting on a particular location may significantly restrict your choice. There are hundreds of firms of solicitors in London but at the last count only six in Penzance itself and only 50 within a 20 mile radius of the town. This means that you will need to make every application count.

You should also remember that in a small community the firms that you apply to are all likely to know each other. Don't tell one firm in your chosen area that you are passionate about tennis and property law and then tell another firm that you are passionate about cross-country running and commercial litigation. They may just compare notes and you'll lose credibility with both.

Foreign travel

Most firms in which this is possible will be either City firms or major regional firms. Some firms second trainees to their foreign offices or to associate firms, but not all firms with foreign offices do so. For some firms this is such an important aspect of building up their global 'brand' that they advertise the number of foreign secondments on their websites. You do not need language skills to be seconded as a trainee, although obviously the ability to speak the lingo will enhance your experience.

If you do indicate that you are interested in foreign travel, you need to be able to have good reasons, such as existing experience working abroad, links with a particular country or ability to speak a relevant language to at least a basic level. A general desire 'to travel', which might be all right if you are applying for a flight crew post, just looks fickle to a law firm.

Being part of a team

This is where you have to take a cold look at yourself and how you like to work. Do you like working with other people? Do you find it productive to share ideas with other people? Are you happier with a single mentor or reporting to large numbers of people? Even large firms have small, tightly knit work teams, but if you are looking for something cosier then consider a smaller firm. Remember that in some larger firms you may find yourself in an open plan office, where your work station will be only semi-partitioned from your colleagues.

Working on your own

In some areas you will be given a substantial amount of responsibility very quickly, which usually means that you will be able to see a complete transaction through from start to finish and be involved with all aspects of the process. In other areas the size of the transaction will be so huge that you should be closely supervised at all times and you may feel that the work that you are being given is unnecessary as someone else will have to do it again anyway.

It's particularly difficult for large firms to give you the former type of experience directly, as most no longer keep residential conveyancing, debt collection and small company matters for their trainees. But on the other hand their trainees may be able to deal with small face-to-face time-bounded matters in pro bono initiatives supported by their firm.

In very small firms you can if you're not careful find yourself out of your depth and be tempted to make judgements that you are not qualified to make. It's a balancing act, but then being a good lawyer is about developing sound judgement not just about learning the law. Only you can judge what would be the most congenial way of working for you.

OTHER BENEFITS

What other benefits are you looking for?

To a large extent a firm's size will dictate the benefits that it can provide, but size is no guarantee that all possible benefits will be on tap. Don't assume that benefits will be provided. If one or more of the following is important to you – then do your research.

Pension contributions

It's perfectly legitimate to ask at what point a firm will give you the opportunity to enter its own pension scheme or will make matching contributions to yours. Asking this is an indication of your ability to take a long-term view and to take charge of your life.

Gym membership

Some of the very largest City firms have their own in-house sports facilities including a swimming pool and aerobic facilities, but many others will provide free or subsidised gym membership. Again, this is a legitimate question; even if a firm intends to make you work 12 hours a day, they like to think that you will spend some of your remaining time keeping sufficiently fit and healthy to cope with their work demands.

Healthcare plan

This is not usually provided by smaller firms to employees. It is offered by many large firms and some of the very large firms also have in-house medical arrangements.

Accessible children's day care or day care vouchers

For most trainees this will not be immediately relevant, but it is one of those little things that are worth noting. Firms may provide childcare vouchers or 'emergency crèche' facilities. While this can obviously be of benefit to all staff, whatever their gender, you can reasonably conclude that firms which have taken the time to consider childcare are likely to be those most concerned about retaining female staff.

Professional development and training

Being a solicitor is a life-long learning experience. The Solictors Regulatory Authority (SRA) has stringent requirements as to the amount of Continuing Professional Development (CPD) hours that you need to put in to maintain your Practising Certificate after qualification. In the hurly-burly of legal life it often seems more important to deal with client work first and CPD second. But if you don't know your stuff, how can you advise clients properly?

Ideally you should be looking for a firm that indicates that it will give you:
- Consistent training during your training contract, whether through hands-on experience, in-house training courses or externally provided courses. The latter two are likely to be easier in large firms, but any solicitor taking on a trainee has real responsibilities towards that trainee in terms of providing depth and variety of experience. Read the material about seat rotation carefully to see if the firm is likely to be able to offer the type of experience that you want.
- Consistent training after qualification. In smaller firms you may have to arrange this yourself, but this is not necessarily a bad thing provided that the firm is willing to pay for it.

Promotion prospects

What is your objective in applying for the training contract? Do you simply want to qualify and then see what happens? Or are you looking for a firm that you feel comfortable with and in which you would like to progress?

It is not unreasonable to ask what the promotion possibilities are within a firm. Some firms advertise that they take on trainees with a view to keeping them on for at least two years after qualification. Others are silent. Some say that a large proportion of their partners were trainees with the firm. Others are silent. Although past performance is no guarantee of future policy, it can give an indication of how the firm is thinking.

If you regularly read the legal press such as *Legal Week, The Lawyer* and the *Gazette* you will begin to get some idea of different firms' retention rates after qualification and after a few years' qualification and also whether they regularly promote partners from solicitors who trained with them. As doing this can take up some little time, this might be a task that you could share with your fellow students.

LOOK AT YOURSELF

Be realistic. And be honest. At some point in your life you will already have had to face the reality of not fitting some standard to get access to a long-cherished ambition. If you are a six foot woman you are never going to be a prima ballerina and if you don't understand maths you can forget about being the next Einstein.

What are your strengths?

■ First write down a list of what you think they are
■ Then ask other people that you trust what they consider to be your strengths and see if they marry up with what you think of yourself

The qualities that you take for granted in yourself may be scarcer and more admired than you think. You may be attracted to court room drama, but your strength may be in teasing out the real meaning of legislation and explaining it simply. You may want an additional challenge, but your core strengths are probably what will get you the job.

Job market strengths

Your job market strengths are an assortment of externally validated assessments and personal qualities. In the first category come educational qualifications and other achievements, whether sporting, cultural or relevant work experience. In the second come what are often defined as 'soft skills' and the things that really interest you.

Educational qualifications

Look carefully at what you've already attained. Don't assume that firms are looking mainly for candidates with law degrees. They know that it will be harder for trainees with non-law degrees to begin with, but also that soon after qualification there will be no discernible difference.

Non-law degrees and other professional qualifications can sometimes be seen as positively advantageous. Surveying for a property firm, accountancy for a corporate or niche tax practice, languages for a strong European firm, medicine or nursing for a medical negligence practice would all be attractive. These are levers – use them!

Unfair as it may seem, you may find that the approach that you take is dictated by your educational qualifications to date and the university that you attended. Don't sink into a slough of despond over this. More than ever lawyers do move around and their careers are not set in stone from the date that they start their training contracts. (One of the top divorce lawyers in the country graduated with a Third.) If you really intend to be a lawyer, your first objective is to get qualified, so look for the firms that are most likely to train you and to give you as much as you want from the beginning.

Source of degree

Although they take pains to point out that they take trainees from a variety of educational institutions and that the diversity ratio has improved, major City firms and some of the large regional firms do seem to take a large number of their trainees from the 'older' universities. It's the clone effect. Many partners themselves come from these universities and it is a 'universal truth' that people quite simply prefer to work with people that they understand or think that they understand because of common values and experiences rather than with people that they think they'll have to work harder to understand and accommodate. The more assured a firm can be that you will 'hit the ground running' then the more likely it is to offer you that all important contract.

The lack of diversity in law firms may begin to change because some international corporate clients are beginning to insist on ethnically diverse legal teams – and are putting their money where their mouths are.

Class of degree

Firsts and 'good' Seconds will be preferred to anything else, but there is a grey area surrounding the relationship of educational institution and class of degree. Would for example a City law firm value a First from one of the newer universities, such as a former polytechnic, as highly as a 'good' Second from an older university? In the absence of appropriate empirical evidence, we couldn't possibly comment...

Larger firms may also go beyond your degree to your A Level results, looking at both the grades and the subjects themselves.

Generally speaking, the higher the class of your first degree the better your chances of obtaining a contract and the more choice that you will have. The lower the class of your degree, the harder you will have to work to obtain a contract, unless you have some other qualification that a firm really wants. Don't give up, but try to match up your ambitions with your proven abilities thus far. And accept that although you may not get a training contract exactly where you want to be now, you could get your first or second job there later. There can be Legal Aid solicitors in Peckham who started in major City firms and property lawyers in City firms who started in Hull.

Mitigating circumstances

If you are determined on a legal career and your educational qualifications do not match up with what the firm states that it requires, consider whether there are any mitigating circumstances which would explain the shortfall in attainment. We are not suggesting that you should invent these, but it may be that at the time of your Finals you had a family bereavement or a serious illness. Alternatively you might have undertaken onerous and responsible jobs at university which, while they contributed to the benefit of the student body, left you with insufficient time for revision. In this category would come being President of the Student Union or Chair of the Debating or University Law Society.

If this is the case, make it clear in a well-presented covering letter and be prepared to provide evidence and references from your lecturers. This does not have to accompany the covering letter, but you should at least have asked your referees, so that they are not taken by surprise by a phone call from the firm concerned.

OTHER ATTRIBUTES

Listening and communication

Every firm will be asking for strong 'communication and listening skills', but firms may interpret the phrase in different ways.

In private practice firms, where you are dealing with people's personal problems, the ability to listen 'between the lines' and then to ask additional and relevant questions is paramount. Other key skills will be the ability to summarise the issues and possible solutions in simple terms and the patience to check whether the client really does understand the problem and the proposed solution.

More corporate practices will be looking for an interest in business and the potential confidence to speak to their clients at a high level. Clarity in presenting suggested solutions to their clients' problems will be highly valued as will the ability to summarise the technical legal background to the advice given to clients. They will also probably be looking for assistance with writing articles and client briefings.

How do you communicate?

Some people prefer to argue on their feet and are extremely adept at this. Others are better at presenting their arguments on paper. Some people are uncomfortable giving snap judgements. Others feel confident about this and thrive on the adrenaline rush. Some people don't mind making mistakes and find it easy to admit them. Others would rather agonise over finding the correct solution than risk being in error.

The most important thing is to be honest with yourself about what kind of person you are. This is certainly where a few honest comments from those you trust will be very useful.

Are you creative or combative?

Would you rather draw up something for a client that will keep him out of trouble or would you rather help him to get out of trouble once he's in it? The first involves negotiating before anything is put on paper and the latter negotiating after the untoward event. The first is 'non-contentious' and the second 'contentious', which involves the possibility of court appearance.

To some extent this depends on whether you are a public or a private person, and it can sometimes be very difficult to assess yourself. This is where the trusted family member or friend comes in.

You also need to assess whether a firm is likely to be biased towards one form of practice or the other. If you have an aversion to contentious work, then a firm with a bias towards medical negligence or matrimonial work may not be for you. However, during your training contract you will have to undertake both contentious and non-contentious work, so it is worth keeping an open mind; what you learn at university and even Law School can be very different from actual practice.

Do you have language skills?

Spanish or Mandarin are more generally useful than Latvian or Turkish, but there may well be a niche practice where such minority languages put you at a distinct advantage. Again, possessing linguistic skills may be a useful lever particularly if you come up short on the educational qualification front.

Do you have knowledge of other cultures?

As more firms become involved in international work and are keen to become big players in the 'global economy' you might find that your gap year in Pakistan or your six months teaching English as a foreign language in Brazil becomes an attractive feature to a law firm. Knowledge and understanding of cultures other than your own is becoming more and more valued.

Do you have musical skills? Sports talents? Acting talent?

Firms might deal with musicians, theatrical companies, football clubs or aspects of the forthcoming Olympic Games. Your Grade VIII piano certificate or your Rugby Blue will not make you more skilled in drawing up contracts for the Royal Opera House or representing an aggrieved rugby player at an Employment Tribunal, but it might make it easier for you to empathise with musical or sporting clients. Remember that the legal life is not just about learning the law; it is also about personal relationships.

What interests you?

What really, really interests you? Be honest with yourself. If you spend all your spare time in outdoor activities, riding, playing golf, fishing or sailing, then working in Portsmouth or in an agriculturally based practice in Norfolk might give you a more satisfying life than working in a large commercial firm in London or Birmingham. Conversely if you are a theatre and cinema nerd, then working in a city will give you more opportunity to indulge your passions. This is not a frivolous consideration, as the more comfortable you are with the rest of your life, the more likely you are to enjoy your work.

What do you expect to get out of your legal career?

Do you see this as a job? Or are you prepared for this to take over your life? Generally speaking you will work longer hours in large, metropolitan firms and shorter ones in High Street firms, but you will be unlikely to earn as much money in the latter. Ask yourself how much you are prepared to give and how much you expect in return.

COMPROMISE

Whichever choice you make will most probably involve compromise. Understand who you are, recognise your strengths and weaknesses and choose where to apply accordingly.

Being a lawyer can be a job, a vocation, a pastime or a life, depending on how much time you devote to it, how important it is to you, the area of law in which you practise and the responsibility you hold in your firm. There are many different cottages and mansions in the law firm village. It's easy to be persuaded that the only place to be is in a City firm earning megabucks, but if that makes you unhappy it is a poor trade-off. Equally if you work in a Legal Aid firm because of your political beliefs but the work does not interest you, that can also be a bad bargain.

On the other hand during your contract you will encounter areas of the law of which you were unaware at university or did not find attractive at Law School. Nothing is certain. Several years after qualifying the physics graduate who thought he would specialise in patent law is a telecoms consultant, the English graduate who intended to be a family lawyer is a tax lawyer and the young graduate who wanted to be an employment lawyer becomes a property developer doing a bit of international contract law on the side.

The best that you can do is to choose a firm that will not exclude your ambitions from the start.

LOVE LETTERS IN THE SAND

And when you have done this, treat every application as a love letter. You'd be careful with that, choosing your words and writing neatly, possibly throwing several drafts in the bin before you sent off the final version. You should treat every application to a law firm in the same way.

It's fine to have a pro forma CV and to have a standard chat-up letter on file, but each application should be meticulously tailored to the firm that you are applying to. This needs to go beyond getting the name and address of the firm correct. You should find out as much as possible about every firm you are applying to and answer every question as if you were reading your reply from their point of view. Why should they employ you? Why would you fit into their firm? Indeed, once you have drafted your application letter, sit back and ask yourself, 'Would I pay for this?'

Chapter 2

APPLYING FOR A TRAINING CONTRACT

SPEED READ SUMMARY

- Application forms must be immaculate. Don't give a law firm the opportunity to reject you because of simple spelling mistakes or poor layout.

- Law firms ask about your other interests because they want to know if you have stamina, can converse with their clients and are a team player.

- Treat applications for Summer Vac placements as seriously as applications for training contracts.

JOINING THE VILLAGE

The first step in becoming a solicitor is to become a member of a law firm village. You do this by making a successful application for a training contract.

YOUR APPLICATION FORM

To get you to the interview stage your application form and letter must be perfect. Look at the criteria that the firm says you must meet. This is usually listed under the 'person specification' for the role of the trainee.

You must meet the criteria with evidence. Many firms do not have Human Resources departments and so you must help them to discriminate. The first sift may be conducted by an administrative assistant or a secretary. So, it is important not to give any silly reason for rejection. If a firm is called 'Bloggs & Smith' addressing the application letter to 'Bloggs and Smith' may well result in an automatic binning of your application. You may think that this is a small thing, but remember that as a lawyer you will have to pay strict attention to detail. Firms may receive hundreds of applications for only five training contracts, so they are looking for easy ways of reducing the application mountain down to a manageable size. Rejecting application forms with spelling and grammatical errors is one way of doing that.

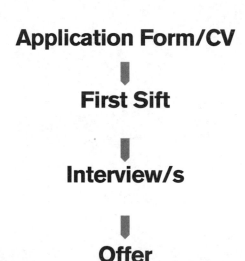

Application Form/CV

First Sift

Interview/s

Offer

Your CV should be printed on white or cream paper. Printing it on green or pink paper will make it stand out, but for all the wrong reasons. And don't head it 'Curriculum Vitae' – it's obvious what it is – but with your name.

Before sending in your application, do a draft. Set it aside. Read it again. Ask as many people as possible whose opinion you value to read it over for easily correctable errors of spelling and grammar. Consult anyone you know who is a partner in a law firm or who has anything to do with recruitment in another organisation. Ask politely if they will look over what you have produced. And listen to them.

Think about what you have done already in your life that may have some relevance to your potential legal life. Firms are looking for achievers. Can you point to anything that will demonstrate your success either by yourself or with others?

SILLY QUESTIONS

Most application forms will contain questions which apparently have nothing to do with the law or your ability to become a lawyer. Why, for example, do you think that legal application forms ask about sporting or other achievements? What relevance does an ability to play netball or cricket have to conveyancing or litigation? What has working on a Water Aid project in Africa got to do with commercial transactions? The answer is that probably none of them will have immediate relevance, but they do have a wider significance.

First, firms are looking for trainees who have a sufficiently wide experience of life that they can speak to clients in a sensible way. Sport is often a good starting-off point. However, there are other topics of conversation, so don't despair if you feel athletically challenged.

Second, many firms are looking for trainees who are fit enough to withstand potential all-nighters and long days when they may be expected to work for ten hours or more and then do some post-work study to get up to speed on some new topic.

Third, firms set great store by 'team-playing'. In large firms in particular, many of whose clients are huge companies conducting deals worth several millions of pounds, it is unlikely that any matter will involve only one lawyer at a time. In such a situation prima donna trainees who cannot communicate with, value the work of and generally get along with other trainees and more senior lawyers will not be at all useful. When you get to your firm you may feel that this analysis is incorrect when you encounter some very stressed and egocentric personalities who are downright rude to support staff, trainees and other lawyers, but remember that this is not what any firm is actually looking for in a trainee. It's just unfortunately what some of their solicitors become.

FIRMS ARE LOOKING FOR TRAINEES WITH:

Other outside interests. This shows that you can manage an academic workload and still have time left to broaden your mind. It also demonstrates an enquiring mind and an ability to get on with other people, particularly clients. Having an interest in theatre, politics, playing sport or acting as a charity trustee suggests to a firm that you have a network of contacts capable of becoming clients at some time in the future, or at least that you are capable of networking at social functions. And it does also indicate that you are capable of juggling competing interests and of managing your time effectively.

Work experience. This could be either directly related to the legal world, which demonstrates commitment to your chosen career, or it could be work undertaken to finance your university and college education. In itself this shows a degree of stamina and determination, but also try to analyse what you learned while you were doing the most menial jobs. If you worked for a fast food outlet, can you describe how you dealt with demanding customers? Did you devise or implement any changes to improve service? Did you have any experience of managing people? Were you promoted? If so, make it clear on your application form.

There is no need to go into great detail about this in the form, but you should describe your experience briefly to show that you were not just the passive recipient of a pay cheque at the end of a week of mind-numbing physical work, but someone who is alert and thoughtful and capable of making a difference to their working environment.

Other experiences. Firms like to feel that they are not hiring clones, even if that is what some of them apparently end up doing. They also like to feel that their trainees are engaged in the world at large. Taking a year off is a plus rather than a minus point, but only if you used it in a 'sensible' way. Spending the year playing tennis round the world would be valued if you were competing in international tournaments, but not if you were moving in a hedonistic haze from one villa to another belonging to your family's friends. Similarly working at almost anything for nothing will be valued more than slobbing around at home because you cannot think of anything else meaningful to do. You must find some positive reasons to have done what you have done and be able to describe some constructive things that you have learned.

This is not entirely duplicitous. One of the skills that you need to acquire as a lawyer is the ability to be persuasive and to argue your client's case successfully whether it is in court, to HM Revenue and Customs or simply to the lawyer 'on the other side'. Before you are allowed to represent clients, you will need to prove that you can do an excellent job of representing yourself.

MAGIC CIRCLE FIRMS

No, these are not rabbit-out-of-the-hat specialists. They are a very small number of large London firms grouped like this because they consistently produce the highest profits per equity partner, are the largest firms and grab the biggest deals. They are Allen & Overy, Clifford Chance, Freshfields Bruckhaus Deringer, Linklaters and Slaughter and May. If you are thinking of applying to any of these firms (or for any of the so-called 'Silver Circle' firms), then special considerations apply.

If you are applying to them it is almost essential to have done a 'Summer Vacation Placement' or have one in place before you apply for your training contract. These firms are swamped with applications and want to be sure that their applicants have had some experience of working in a law firm, preferably a City of London law firm, before choosing law as a career. If you are considering a Summer Vacation Placement with one of these firms, you should write to them for an application form, but check first with their website to see whether they will accept only applications submitted online.

Remember that exactly the same considerations about the accuracy, layout and thoughtfulness of the initial letter and the completion of the application for the Summer Vacation Placement are as relevant as when you complete the application form for your real training contract.

And because Summer Vacation Placements are now so competitive, some firms even interview their candidates for such placements. If you are asked for interview, treat it very seriously indeed, because if nothing else it is practice for the real thing.

SUMMER BENEFITS

Firms other than Magic Circle firms also offer Summer Vacation Placements, and even if you are not considering a Magic Circle training contract it is worth considering such a placement for the following reasons:

- They can be very well paid. In London you can earn £400 to £500 per week. Placements are usually for two or more weeks and you could be fortunate enough to obtain more than one during the summer period.

- You get to participate in the social life of the firm. You may be invited to client functions, to play in departmental or firm sporting evenings and often there are social evenings arranged just for the vacation students. But read Chapter 12 and Chapter 15 before you participate too fully.

- You will get some understanding of how a legal office works. Your experience of actual legal work will depend very much on how busy your supervisors are, what sort of work the department to which you are allocated does and how sensitive the clients are. You may be invited to client meetings, asked to take notes or to do research, or sometimes just generally to 'mooch around'. Don't be offended if your work is not relied on. That's not the purpose of your being there. Your being there costs the firm money, so make the most of their generosity and learn as much as you can. This will save you time when it comes to your 'real' training time.

- It may lead to the offer of a formal training contract. This would be a bonus but don't be too disappointed if it does not. If your Summer Vac firm does not offer you such a contract as it bids you farewell at the end of your time with them, don't let this put you off applying to them. You will after all have a better idea than many other applicants about how the firm works and what they are looking for.

If you are successful in obtaining a summer placement, then read the rest of this book very carefully before you go. For these few weeks you are training to be a trainee.

Chapter 3

BEING INTERVIEWED FOR YOUR TRAINING CONTRACT

SPEED READ SUMMARY

- Firms assess you on your paper applications, by telephone and ultimately in a face-to-face interview. Take every element of the process very seriously.

- HR professionals know what the firm is looking for, so listen very carefully to their advice.

- Do your research before an interview. Your chosen subjects are yourself and the firm you are applying to. Prepare yourself to avoid the things you can get wrong in an interview. You need to sell yourself through experience, manner and positive attitude.

- Take care of the obvious things within your control such as punctuality, appearance and body language.

- Interviewers adopt a variety of questioning techniques. Make sure you are ready for difficult and downright illegal questions.

- A good contract involves a willing buyer and a willing seller. If you are offered a contract, check that its terms fit with your expectations.

- If you don't get an offer, ask for feedback and use it to help you at the next interview.

The selection process can take many forms and can have many stages: initial paper sift, telephone interviews, face-to-face interviews and assessment days involving role plays, team exercises and psychometric testing. Here we focus on face-to-face interviews but much of the advice is equally applicable to telephone interviews or assessment interviews. Whatever the format, you need to have prepared beforehand. Recognise your strengths, work out how to cover your weaknesses and anticipate difficult questions.

NOT QUITE THE INTERVIEW

Many firms, and particularly the larger ones, operate a two-tier interview system. The first level is the interview with someone from the HR department; if you get through that you will be invited back for a second interview with the partners. Do not make the mistake of taking this first interview less seriously than you would an interview with a lawyer. Experienced HR professionals will have a very good idea of what their firms are looking for, and although they will not be asking you tricky questions about current legal issues, they can be adept at winkling out the fantasy from the reality of your claim that you are a devotee of the theatre or that you are fluent in three different languages.

They will check through your CV with you, ask you to expand certain aspects of it and generally make a note of your dress and demeanour. You will most certainly be asked why you want to be a lawyer. So make sure that you have really thought about this and have a positive answer to the question, even if you are in fact trying to decide between the law and becoming a butcher. In fact all the comments in the rest of this chapter apply equally to the interview with HR.

AND AGAIN NOT QUITE THE INTERVIEW...

At some point in the proceedings you may have an opportunity to have a cup of tea or even lunch with current trainees or associates. This will be presented to you as your chance to ask what it is really like to be employed by the firm. What sort of work will you get? What provision is there for ongoing training? What hours do they expect you to work? What social life is there? What are the overseas offices like?

If you join in the conversation and think about the answers and the way that they are given you can glean a fair amount of information not only about the way that the firm treats its junior staff, but also about the sort of

Preparation

Your objectives will be easier to achieve if you prepare properly. Make a preparation checklist. You should:

- Research the firm on the internet and get hold of their publicity material
- Read the job description/role profile carefully (training contracts vary enormously)
- Reread your CV (are there any gaps or anomalies to explain?)
- Work out where to go and how to get there – leave plenty of extra time in case of emergencies
- Make a good first impression – hair cut and styled/suit dry cleaned/shoes polished and reheeled/clean nails/ subtle accessories
- Prepare to 'sell yourself' without appearing pushy
- Anticipate questions – if the interview is being run properly questions will relate to a proper set of transparent selection criteria

junior staff you will be working and socialising with. Don't try to confine the conversation to fact-finding. After all, it's their lunch-break too. And remember that this is a two-way information street. You may be learning more about the firm in a less formal setting, but the firm is also learning more about you.

It is likely that your lunch companions will be asked for their brief impressions of you. So, don't be silent, but don't be boastful, don't swear, don't make too appreciative comments about the receptionists (male or female) and if you are having lunch after a partner interview don't comment critically about the person who interviewed you. If alcohol is on offer, drink moderately if at all, and mind your table manners.

THE PURPOSE OF AN INTERVIEW

Your interviewers should be aiming to establish a good rapport with you in order to obtain the information which will help them to decide whether to offer you a position. Your objective is almost the same, save that you may have to decide whether to take the position when it is offered. Even though it is a buyer's market, because law firms have their pick of LPC graduates, you should remember that the interview is not just your opportunity to sell yourself, but also your opportunity to assess the people you might soon be working with.

ARRIVE IN GOOD TIME

Time is money for busy lawyers, many of whom bill several hundred pounds an hour. If you turn up late, it may cost them where it hurts and they will not thank you for it. To you the interview may have a life-changing significance, but it will be only one meeting of a great many that day for your interviewers. This does not mean that they will not take it seriously, simply that they may be squeezing you in between client appointments and tight deadlines to be met. Make sure that they keep you waiting, not the other way round.

Arriving early also gives you the time to acclimatise yourself to your surroundings and to sit quietly composing yourself. Look around. Observe. You can learn a lot about a firm by sitting in its reception area for 15 minutes. Bring as little else to the interview as possible. If you do have to bring two suitcases and a shopping bag because you are going home for the weekend, ask the receptionist whether you can leave them with her until you leave. You simply will not look or feel professional manoeuvring luggage into lifts and along narrow corridors.

Sometimes a secretary will take you to the interview room, sometimes it will be a partner or an assistant solicitor. When someone comes to collect you, stand up immediately, smile and make eye contact. Look pleased to be there but don't be effusive. Don't try too hard to be liked. Remember that this is business not pleasure. You are aiming to earn respect, not to be someone's best friend. Take the lead from the person who collects you. If you are invited to shake hands, do so firmly but not with hand-crushing vigour, and try to maintain eye contact.

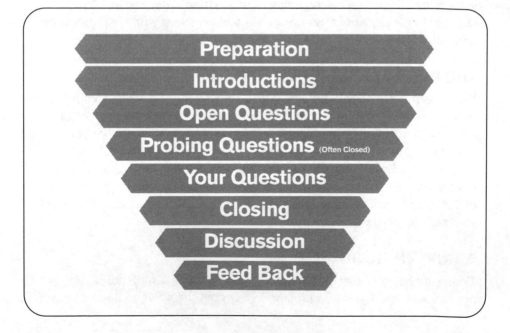

FIRST IMPRESSIONS

When you come for your first interview with a firm, be polite, smile and explain clearly why you are there. Be polite to the receptionists, but not too chatty. They are trained to see right through that.

If you wait for your interview in the reception area, don't fidget, but appear as though you are doing something constructive, like reading the *Financial Times* and not the *Sun*. Unless you are desperate for a caffeine slug, it's probably a good idea to decline, politely, any proffered cup of coffee. If you are a little early, you will then have an opportunity for a little covert observation of what they do and how they behave. You may also be able to gather information about whether this is a firm that you would want to join.

In many offices receptionists are often asked informally for their impressions of candidates for training contracts or new appointments. Remember this facet of being a 'team player'. Receptionists are part of the firm's team and in a unique position to observe all the firm's fee-earners, clients and potential employees.

WHAT TO EXPECT

There is not much that you can predict about an interview, and paradoxically the more successful you have been at getting the university and vacation jobs of your choice the less experience you will have had of different types of interview.

Interviews should have a beginning, a middle and an end. There should be a greeting when you arrive (but even that might be hard to spot), questions for you to answer, then a period when the interview is brought to a close.

Interviewers frequently fail to introduce themselves. If that is the case there is not much you can do at the time since to ask, even politely, at the start might make you look somewhat pushy. This is something that you should check later with the receptionist or on the internet if the firm publishes staff photos, so that you remember who was who if you later accept a training contract with the firm.

The questioning phase, when you are on the hot spot, is dealt with below in detail. The drawing to a close phase should involve inviting you to ask any questions that you have (it is always good to have two or three to show you are interested) and then telling you what will happen next and when. If the interview appears to be ending and you are not invited to ask questions, ask politely if you may ask some and, most importantly, make sure to find out what will happen next in the recruitment process.

ENVIRONMENTAL DIFFICULTIES AND HOW TO DEAL WITH THEM

The interview should take place in an environment which will help rather than hinder effective communication but if the sunlight is shining directly in your eyes or the room is so warm that you begin to feel drowsy, then you should say something. Ask politely if the blind could be drawn or a window could be opened for a little air. The interviewers should not mind. They should be aiming to create an atmosphere in which you can feel calm and relaxed.

Sometimes interviewers set up rooms with the intention of making the interviewee feel ill at ease. You will not know this of course, and if you are uncomfortable you should still ask if blinds could be closed or whether you could move your chair. It may well have been a test of whether you are mature enough to take at least momentary charge of a situation. Deliberately trying to make interviewees physically uncomfortable is counterproductive since interviewees are more likely to be themselves when relaxed but unfortunately not all interviewers think this way. If you feel that you are being manipulated, you should ask yourself whether if you have a choice, you would really like to work for this firm.

Lawyers have demanding clients, so be prepared for interruptions from telephone calls, Blackberries ringing or people coming and going. Just take the interruptions in your stride, your interviewer will probably be apologetic anyway. Don't allow your mind to drift off. Remain focused and use the interruption to prepare an answer to the question you have just been asked or to rehearse the questions you are going to ask at the end of the interview.

SEATING ARRANGEMENTS

Sometimes you will be put in front of a row of interviewers, as if before a firing squad, without so much as a table in front of you as protection. On other occasions you will be invited into a room to sit around a boardroom-style table. In this case, try to choose one of the long sides of the table so that you are opposite the interviewers and able to talk to them square on.

If the seating arrangements are more relaxed, comfy armchairs around a fire even, you should remember to remain formal, alert and professional in your approach. Sit up and don't slouch and watch your body language. Legs splayed and an arm casually flopping over the back of the chair give the wrong impression.

GETTING DOWN TO IT

We all have weak points in our interviewing style but we can try to modify them. Even before you get to the interview you can maximise your chances of being successful. Get a friend or colleague whom you trust to give you a mock interview on the understanding that they give you fair and honest feedback afterwards, and that you will not hold their comments against them.

Ask yourself, and get your friend to tell you, if you commit any of these common gaffes at interview:
■ Talking too much and thus not recognising when the interviewer has lost interest or wants to speak
■ Failing to listen properly (not the same as talking too much)
■ Jumping in prematurely before the interviewer has finished asking the question
■ Demonstrating a lack of understanding about the organisation, for example by asking questions that were readily answerable if you had bothered to look at their website
■ Avoiding a question rather than giving a straight answer or saying 'I don't know'
■ Talking too quietly, too quickly, mumbling or frequently using fillers such as 'You know' or 'I mean'

ACTIVE LISTENING

One of the most important techniques to master is 'active listening'. You listen actively when you show the person who is speaking not only that you understand what they are saying but also how they are thinking and feeling.

You can show this by:
■ Maintaining good eye contact (this does not mean staring fixedly). If you are being interviewed by two people, one may be the main interviewer asking all the questions. Remember to maintain eye contact with both, otherwise one of them may feel irritated. It's a sign that you would be able to engage all clients in a meeting.
■ Occasionally summarising back what the other person has said before answering the question.

- Reflecting back feelings or thoughts.
- Not actually saying anything but nodding and making 'mmm' noises as appropriate. However, don't overdo this or you will come across like a nodding dog.

Behaving like this naturally and not in a forced way will help you to establish a rapport with the interviewers. This is important because even if you give good answers, you probably won't score highly overall if you are marked down for not being able to build rapport with others, otherwise known as 'people skills'.

SILENCE

Watch out for periods of silence in the interview. Your interviewers may well be making notes or thinking about what you have just said or even formulating the next question. Don't be frightened by it or feel awkward and definitely don't jump in and start babbling just to fill up the space. Be conscious of your and their body language.

POOR BODY LANGUAGE AND MANNERISMS

Most of us are not even aware of our poor body language habits or distracting mannerisms. Watching a video of yourself giving a short talk can be quite revealing. If you can't arrange this, then a trusted friend could help you to look constructively at the visual impression you give when talking with other people.

Did you do any of the following?
- Tap your feet
- Jiggle your feet
- Fiddle with or chew your pen
- Twiddle with your hair
- Stare fixedly without breaking eye contact
- Laugh or giggle nervously
- Chew your nails
- Tap or drum your fingers
- Slouch
- Clear your throat repeatedly
- Grind your teeth

These traits can be so distracting for interviewers that they may fail to get down something important that you say or they may even give up trying to listen to you altogether. Before the interview do what you can to eliminate these habits, or at least remove the temptation to indulge in them. Practise sitting still, get a new hair cut or style, suck a throat lozenge before the interview and avoid drinks like tea and coffee which can dry your throat.

REFRESHMENTS

The safest thing to accept is a glass of water. It lubricates the throat, keeps you going if the interview goes on for a long time, and avoids the embarrassment of your feeling that you have to gulp down cold coffee or tea at the end of the interview because you have been too busy talking to drink it. A glass of water is also much easier to manipulate than a cup and saucer, especially if they come accompanied with a biscuit. If your mouth goes dry and you have no water, gently and without making it obvious, pinch your tongue between your front teeth for a few seconds. Try it, it really works.

PRESENTATIONS

As part of the interview process you may be invited to make a presentation. The firm will be using this as a means of identifying the candidates who can research a given topic, express themselves clearly and answer questions confidently. As with the rest of the interview, the key word is 'preparation'.

Practise your presentation beforehand and, whatever you do, keep it to time. Interviewers soon grow tired of listening to the same topic covered umpteen times (even if the approaches are different) so don't run over time. Support your presentation with an accurate, error-free written note or handout. Use technology (e.g. MS PowerPoint) only if you are completely comfortable using it and only if the technology is easy to set up and you have checked beforehand that it is OK for you to use it. If you waste ten minutes of your allotted time (or more importantly of the panel's precious time) fiddling with a laptop or projector before you even start, you will not make a good impression.

QUESTIONING TECHNIQUES

Some interviewers have had some training in questioning techniques; others simply rely on the skills they have learned from practice. You will most likely be asked a mixture of 'open' and 'closed' questions.

Open questions do not invite a Yes or No response, but invite you to be more expansive. Open questions have the advantage that they allow you to select the answer and give the information you believe to be relevant. Remember though that their disadvantage is that you might start to ramble or get off the point or provide irrelevant information. You need to keep a careful eye on the interviewing panel to try to read from their expressions whether they are satisfied that you have answered the question.

If you are not sure that you have understood the question properly, it is perfectly reasonable to repeat it back or to paraphrase it before you start to respond. Don't however do this with every question.

Closed questions on the other hand give you a limited set of responses, sometimes even as limited as yes or no. They are sometimes used by interviewers as they hurriedly check through your CV looking for their next good question, 'I see you went to Thinkalot School?' 'And you are 23?'

However, a question such as 'Did you do pro bono work at university?' although apparently an example of a closed question is really in two parts. If the answer is yes, you should continue with a (very) short description of what you actually did.

Closed questions are useful from the interviewers' point of view because they allow them to pinpoint issues and save time. They may even be used to restrict a verbose interviewee. The disadvantage is that you might feel the interview is rather clinical and if you are not careful it could deprive you of the chance to explain and really sell yourself.

LEADING QUESTIONS

Be prepared for conflict in an interview. Some interviewers will use the opportunity to test your mettle, justifying it on the basis that in practice you will need to be able to respond to a counter-argument. You might even be cross-examined; some questions may appear hostile or seek to undermine what you have just said. This type of question is often a **leading question** i.e. it contains the answer in the question itself.

'You haven't studied commercial law in any great detail, have you?'

Stand your ground. Remember that you don't have to agree with the proposition put forward in a leading question. Also tell the truth. Experienced lawyers have learned to spot a lie a mile off. Your truthful and positive answer might be, 'That's true, but I'm confident that if necessary I could get up to speed on it very quickly.'

TRICKY QUESTIONS

Some of the hardest questions to answer may require you to say or imply something negative about yourself. How would you answer one of these questions?

- Can you describe a situation in which you failed at something?
- What do you find most difficult about work?
- What is your biggest weakness?
- Can you describe a situation where you were in conflict with another person?

You need to be prepared for questions like these. You can admit to shortcomings, because everyone has them and the panel would soon see through you if you tried to imply that you were perfect, but you should also think of ways of showing yourself in an attractive light because you have recognised your failures and demonstrated that you have learned from them.

'My father was a very good swimmer, and he thought that I would learn to swim naturally if he simply threw me in the sea. Well, it didn't work. I can remember being humiliated and terrified. But when I was much older I paid for swimming lessons and I am now a fairly competent swimmer.'

'Work can become too absorbing. I've had to learn that if I take proper breaks I can work more effectively.'

'My biggest weakness is probably that I can be stubborn, with a very strong desire to prove I am right, but I have learned to be a better listener and to look for the optimum way to resolve a dispute.'

'Recently I was involved in a dispute with a retailer regarding a sofa that I had purchased over the internet. The colour was not as advertised. I was entitled to a full refund which the retailer was refusing to give. In the end we negotiated a settlement – I kept the sofa and they gave me a substantial discount off a bookcase.'

Make sure that you have really thought about these and that you can answer subsequent questions. 'So how far can you swim?' 'How long should a reasonable break be?' 'Don't you ever give in?' 'Didn't you give in too easily – why didn't you insist on a refund?'

ILL-ADVISED OR ILLEGAL QUESTIONS

Sometimes interviewers ask questions that offend equal opportunities policies and legislation, for example by putting questions that would suggest they discriminate against a particular group of applicants, such as working parents.

- Do you intend to have children?
- When would you see yourself starting a family?
- What is your family situation – do you have children?
- How will you manage with any work-related travel if you have children?
- What happens when your childcare responsibilities clash with work and client priorities?

You are within your rights not to answer any question, including the above, if you don't want to. These should not be asked and used as criteria for giving you the job or not. However, there are occasions when you can turn these questions to your advantage, but only if you address them with 100% confidence.

'Even though you are not supposed to ask me that, I'll answer the question because it might be helpful for you to know that my mother lives round the corner, my children love going on activity holidays and I have a fully equipped home office so that I can work from home.'

If the question is unspoken, but you sense it is hanging in the air, you should assess whether it is better to say something rather than to leave it hanging. Only address it if you can do so with total confidence.

'Even though you have not asked me this, and I appreciate it, I thought that you would like to know that I have two children and that they are looked after by my full-time nanny. I am the main breadwinner, and my career is of paramount importance.'

Before you go into the interview anticipate these questions, spoken or unspoken, and decide what line you are going to take. If you do not want to answer them (your circumstances might not be as helpful as those described above) state simply, 'I believe that I do not have to answer this question, and I am sure that you would not base a decision on whether to employ me or not on my family circumstances. I can assure you that I shall always act in a professional way.' Remember that you should not have to justify being a working parent, but sometimes it can positively help to do so.

And if they ask whether you would put your family before the firm, turn it round. 'In the unlikely event that I would have to choose, ultimately I would always put my family before work. But then wouldn't anybody?' If that gets a stony-faced response, think twice before working for this firm.

OTHER NO-GO QUESTIONS

There are now whole areas of questioning which would potentially fall foul of recent and proposed anti-discrimination legislation. Again you are entirely within your rights to refuse to answer them, but it would be wise to think about these questions before your interview in case you are faced with well-intentioned but not very experienced interviewers, who have not fully thought through the implications of what they are asking.

Finding a way to answer these questions without taking a hostile stance is a significant challenge, but if you can do so it puts the ball in your court. After all, the name of the game is to be offered a training contract. You can always turn down the offer of a contract, perhaps with a short but polite note of explanation if a line of questioning during interview has suggested that your future progress may be hampered by inherent discriminatory attitudes.

The aim of the anti-discrimination legislation is to ensure that employers assess all their employees and potential employees on the basis of their actual or potential performance, not on the basis of gender, ethnicity, disability, age, religion or sexual preferences. Experienced HR interviewers have suggested to us that the following dubious questions would be better not asked:

Any question which relates to ethnicity and nationality, such as:

- Is English your native language? However, if you feel that your ability to speak one or more languages other than English fluently would be advantageous to the firm, then you might already have indicated this on your application form.
- Where were your parents born?
- Do you have the right to work in the UK? If you are offered a training contract, this will have relevance, but it should not be asked of candidates at interview.

Any question which relates to religious background or affiliation

If you are however offered a contract it might be wise to explain that your religion has certain requirements. This might arise, for instance, if you are

Jewish and need to leave the office early in the winter months in order to comply with Sabbath laws.

Any questions about marital status, children and career breaks

(Although we have outlined how these might be dealt with above.)

Questions about your sexual orientation

Questions about your age

- There should be no requirement to disclose your age or date of birth on your application form. An astute interviewer should be able to form some idea of your age from the educational qualifications and work experience set out in your application. After all, you are not going to have a first degree and a Ph.D in Information Technology, five years' experience at IBM, six years working in Australia as a dive instructor and another four years on your family farm before turning to the law, if you are only 25.
- How long do you intend to stay with the firm? This should not be asked of any potential trainee, but if addressed to an older candidate can potentially offend against the age discrimination legislation.

Questions concerning disability and illness

- How would your disability affect your ability to do your job? You should not be rejected solely on the grounds of any perceived disability, and if offered a training contract your employer has a responsibility to make what are called 'reasonable adjustments' to make your work possible. Take encouragement as people can make successful careers in the law despite substantial disabilities.

Questions about 'lifestyle choices'

This covers the 'vice' area of alcohol, recreational drugs and smoking. The smoking question is to some extent irrelevant as you will not be permitted to smoke in the office. Overindulgence in anything that impairs your work performance whether as a trainee or a fully qualified solicitor will probably result in your being shown the door, but at interview you do not have to disclose your preference for drink-related oblivion every weekend. Remember though that firms may have a drug and/or drink testing policy before and during employment. They have a responsibility to their clients not to have their work done by befuddled trainees or solicitors.

COMMERCIAL AWARENESS QUESTIONS

To some extent all firms, but certainly the large, commercial ones, are particularly interested in whether their potential trainees have some degree of what is termed 'commercial awareness'. Although interpreted differently this essentially means an interest in business and how the law can be applied for the benefit of business clients.

If you are interviewed while still at university, and especially if you are a non-law undergraduate, it may be difficult for you to speak with any authority on detailed aspects of case law or legislation, but you could impress by showing some understanding not only of what an M&A is for example but of what M&A work the firm has recently been involved in.

Reading Chris Stoakes' book, *All You Need to Know about Commercial Awareness* (see **Useful Books**, *p.229*) will go a long way to getting you clued up to answer questions on this topic.

SELLING YOURSELF

You are going to have to sell yourself to the interview panel if you want to get the job. Banish from your mind any notions about hard selling (fast-talking, hoodwinking sales people in nasty suits). You may be subtle, controlled and honest and you may be wearing an impressive new suit but, make no mistake, you are going to sell.

The selling mantra

Features describe. Benefits sell. A woman wants to buy a dress. The one she buys is size 12, is blue, is mid-calf length, has a V neck. These are all features of the dress but these features alone will not sell the dress.

When she decides to buy it is because of the benefits the dress will give her. It makes her look slim, it is in this season's colour and cut and makes her feel fashionable. In short it gives her confidence and she simply feels good in it.

Imagine you are describing yourself to a prospective employer. You need to get across not only your qualifications and experience (your features) but also what you can actually do for the firm (the benefits of employing you). For example a solicitor being interviewed for a post in litigation might highlight personal features and benefits by saying 'I have lots of advocacy experience through pro bono work which means that I would be able to do advocacy for the firm's clients if required to, thereby giving them a seamless service'.

Before your interview sit down with your CV (your features) and then draw up a list of the benefits you bring. Look at each item in your CV and your past experience and see whether you can translate them into future benefits for your potential employer. If you have trouble getting started, then use the wording below to list each of your attributes and achievements and then deduce how they could be used for the benefit of an employer.

I am/I can/I have...

which means .... for the firm

YOUR TURN

When it comes to the part when you are invited to ask questions, don't be embarrassed to refer to notes you made earlier. It shows that you cared enough to do your preparation and to write down the things that were important to you. Equally don't be embarrassed to make very brief notes of their answers. A good lawyer always makes notes. If necessary, probe further by asking supplementary questions for clarification, but be careful not to put the interviewers on the defensive with leading or pointed questions such as 'You don't have many female partners do you?' You may well blow your chances if you make the interviewer feel uncomfortable. Instead probe gently with more open questions such as:

- Can you explain your partnership structure in a little more detail?
- I was wondering what you meant by the comprehensive induction programme?
- What opportunities are there to... ?
- Can you tell me more about your foreign internship programme?

However, make sure that you know the answers to any 'technical' questions before you ask them. If you are going to ask about their partnership structure you should, for example, know what a limited liability partnership (or LLP) is. Don't ask questions about things that you could have found out by looking at the firm's website, and don't ask questions that some partners may not be able to answer without asking HR. If you are being interviewed by a Commercial Litigation partner, a question about the number of trainees in the Property department will be profoundly irritating.

IF YOU GET THE JOB

This is your last chance for a while for a drink at the negotiating saloon.

The opening gambit (their first offer) in this negotiation will not usually occur at the interview stage. It will probably come later in a letter from the firm or even a phone call from its HR department. But whenever it comes, be prepared.

Be clear about what you are being offered, in other words what is on the table for negotiation. The key things to watch out for are salary (basic and bonus), holiday allowance, hours of work, start date, place of work (some firms have more than one office) and how long the offer is open to you.

CAN TRAINEES NEGOTIATE?

As a potential trainee it is unlikely that there will be much room for negotiation, but you should at least be sure that the offer terms are clear. Ambiguities might seem trivial or unimportant but they have a nasty habit of coming back to bite you if you let them go now. If you think that you are going to be working in Reading but they want you to work in Birmingham, that could make a big difference to your living arrangements. In such circumstances it would not be unreasonable to ask for a relocation allowance or, if it means a long commute, whether your start times could fit in with your train times.

The extent to which you are able to negotiate really depends on whether you have alternatives to accepting this job offer. If you hold another offer then you are in a strong position and can sometimes play one off against the other, though not necessarily overtly. For example you can go back to your least favourite offer and ask (in a polite way) if one or more aspects of the offer can be improved. If you have another and better offer, you have nothing to lose.

Salary is the trickiest component to improve as most firms offer a standard starting salary to their trainees and newly qualified associates. Generally they will be unwilling to pay one new trainee or new associate more than the others because any leaking of the pay differential will lead to widespread grumbling. If, however, you are the only trainee or newly qualified solicitor that your firm is taking on, you could be in a stronger position to negotiate over salary. Whatever you ask for, know why you are asking for it – be able to justify the request with objective reasons if necessary.

Don't forget that the features and benefits that made them want to offer you the job may mean that they want you more than you want them. If they have Japanese clients your fluency in Japanese may make you highly desirable. But don't overestimate your worth – you could end up with nothing if you negotiate badly with those who have made offers.

In this situation, as so often in life, information is priceless. The starting salary is not the end of the story, merely the first chapter in a long saga. Various organisations vie with each other to present up-to-date comparative tables on legal salaries which includes trainee starting salaries, as well as salaries for newly qualified, one year qualified, two year qualified and three year qualified. After that firms tend to differentiate. Take a look at websites rollonfriday.com or totallylegal.com for up-to-date comparisons and information.

CRITERIA FOR CHOICE

Though you might at times feel that any job would be great, you should think about how to discriminate between prospective employers and the jobs offered to you.

It is important to decide what it is that you personally want and what criteria you are going to use in order to 'score' jobs and employers. Go back to the list that you made before you applied (in Chapter 1) of all the things that would together add up to an ideal work situation for you.

- Check the facts of any offers against the list of priorities that you made initially.
- Remind yourself what bits of your ideal specification you were willing to trade to get other bits which you consider non-negotiable. You might for example be willing to trade salary for flexibility, or to undertake a longer commute in order to work in a niche shipping practice where there is abundant foreign travel.
- Then rank the offers in the order in which they satisfy your initial criteria. Now stand back and ask yourself whether your compromise position is still the same. If it isn't, then why not?
- You may have realised that no amount of money can persuade you to spend four hours a day travelling to and from work. You may have decided that although your engineering qualification would fit well with an IP firm, you really are no longer interested in that area.
- The interview process itself may have altered your ideal job criteria, simply because you have found one group of interviewers more sympathetic than another. This is not an invalid reason for choosing one

firm over another, although remember that in a large firm you may never meet any of these sympathetic (or unsympathetic) interviewers again.

Ask yourself whether your original criteria were inappropriate or whether you are now being influenced by the halo effect of having had a pleasant time in the interview room. If you are going to jettison something that you thought was immensely important to you, then try to find out more about the firm before you accept their offer.

Be honest with yourself.

IF YOU DON'T GET THE JOB

Your first reaction may be to consign the rejection letter to the waste-basket and to move on. However, any feedback you can obtain is enormously helpful, even when it feels uncomfortable or disappointing to have to ask for it following an unsuccessful interview. Feedback can help you to refocus and make your next application more successful. To make it as useful as possible, remember these simple rules:

■ Don't be afraid to ask for it
■ Explain why you have made the request
■ Don't use it as a way of reopening an unsuccessful application
■ Try to avoid arguing back or criticising the person giving feedback
■ Remember to thank the person who has taken time to give you the feedback
■ Keep an open mind
■ Focus on the 'transferable' feedback that will help you to find a job; don't get stuck on the employer/job-specific feedback

Above all remember that the interviewers are looking for someone to fit into 'their' firm. Don't take their rejection as a sign of failure. It wasn't a viva for a university degree, it was simply a date that didn't work out. Or to put it another way, the villagers didn't think that you'd fit in and maybe you wouldn't have been happy living there anyway. Look objectively at their comments, discuss them with a friend, put them together with your own impressions of how the interview went and work out how you might present yourself even more effectively for the future, so that it is you who will be making the choices.

Chapter 4

WHAT A TRAINING CONTRACT MEANS

SPEED READ SUMMARY

- A training contract is a special sort of employment contract. You are there to be of use to the firm as well as to be trained.

- Make the most of training sessions by preparing for them and revising afterwards.

- All your work should be supervised, but the amount of teaching time you receive will depend on the experience and availability of your supervisor.

- You need helpful feedback in order to improve. Ask for it.

What you sign with your employing firm is called a training contract. You may well, and quite reasonably, assume that this means that the firm is binding itself to train you, and that this is therefore the point of the contract that you have just signed. But contrary to what you may think, and what you will just have experienced on the LPC, your training is not the primary purpose of your relationship with the firm. In reality it is a special kind of employment contract, with a requirement that at the end of your training contract the firm will certify that you are fit to be employed by it or by another firm. It is as well to bear that in mind.

Back when firms charged trainees a premium for their training the relationship was different. It did not mean that the supervisor did any more training than now, but it did mean that the supervisor was not so concerned if an articled clerk took the odd afternoon off or took a very long time returning from the law courts. Now that firms pay their trainees this has changed. As a trainee you will probably receive a multiple of what many of your graduate contemporaries are earning and you don't get that sort of money for nothing.

Do not be under any illusions. The essence of the training contract is not that the firm should train you, but that you should be of use to the firm. They are paying you to perform, and they expect to get some value for their money.

FORMAL TRAINING

If the firm is a conscientious one, and even more so if it is a large one, it will arrange classes for its trainees that give them access to skills and knowledge training. Trainees will also be expected to attend departmental training sessions on new developments in the law or participate in role-play sessions to improve their client-relationship skills. Don't be put off because you feel that the topics under discussion are over your head. Many of the other solicitors will be feeling the same, they just don't admit it.

Don't skip these sessions. You may just learn something, and your non-attendance will be noted and may be used against you when you are applying to stay on at your firm at the end of your contract. They may also bring you into contact with trainees and solicitors in other departments which will help you to get a flavour of the character and scope of those departments. You may find that some or even all of these sessions will be arranged in the evenings and at the weekends. There is no point in being aggrieved about this. You chose the firm and could have asked about their training policy when you interviewed them.

To get the most benefit out of your firm's training sessions, take them seriously:

■ Try to find ten minutes beforehand to ask yourself what you really know about the discussion topic.

■ Keep all handouts whether electronically or in hard copy. Supervisors have a nasty habit of almost remembering something that they heard in such a session and asking you to find the information or reference for them. If both of you have dumped the handouts in the waste-paper bin, you could spend a lot of time locating the details required.

■ Some of the points discussed during training may come up in practice, although remember that the law or practice may have moved on by the time you come to use them. Always do your own research and check the up-to-date position.

■ Trainees are sometimes asked to make presentations; it's part of your training for helping to train others in the future and most importantly for marketing to clients. If you have a choice, keep the topic as narrow and focused as possible, not 'Capital Gains Tax on Residential Property' but 'Capital Gains Tax on Main Residences when Let' or 'Capital Gains Tax on Main Residences Owned Jointly by Family Members'. Anticipate the questions that you might be asked, prepare brief answers to them and also simple handouts. A page outlining the main points of your talk will do.

SUPERVISION

After years of various forms of education you will be familiar with the concepts of 'teacher', 'lecturer' and 'tutor'. Although your relationship with your new employer is defined as a training contract, the people with whom you will become most familiar will be 'supervisors'.

A supervisor is literally someone whom you 'sit with' and who is meant to check your work. Supervisors will refer to you as 'my trainee', or as 'Joe Bloggs' trainee', often in a proprietary way. Your supervisor usually has first call on your time, and it is usually considered courteous for your supervisor to be asked first if another qualified solicitor wants to 'borrow' you to help with some work.

SITTING WITH A PARTNER OR AN ASSISTANT

Some firms have a policy of assigning trainees only to partners. Because partners may be engaged in one massive matter at a time, you may find that your experience of a particular department is very narrow. As tight deadlines approach, your supervising partner may have very little time to answer questions which to you are momentous, but to someone who has been asked them so many times before may seem entirely trivial.

At other times you may find yourself sitting with an assistant solicitor who has been qualified for only two or three years. When you yourself have reached that stage of qualification you will realise just how little knowledge and experience that may actually mean. Although for now there is a mountain of difference between you, you may be fortunate enough to find yourself sitting with someone who can remember how difficult it was being a trainee and who has the same sort of social life as you – although rather better funded.

In larger firms it is common for partners to take assistants and trainees to meetings with them. This can be very advantageous, because you get the opportunity to listen to the partner and the assistant discussing the client's business and also the opportunity, if the assistant is not too harassed, to talk the issues over afterwards in your shared room.

Don't think that because you are sitting with an assistant and not a partner you are somehow being devalued. This is not the case. You may find yourself obtaining far more varied experience, not least because other fee-earners who are looking for additional assistance will often focus on the trainee of the fee-earner with the least status in the department.

If you do find yourself supervised by an assistant rather than a partner, do not treat it as the soft option. He or she may be closer to you in age than a partner would be, may share similar interests to you outside work and may get quite pally, but your relationship is still one of unequals. Your aim is to be respected for your hard work and your ability – being popular won't hurt, but of itself it won't be enough.

GETTING FEEDBACK

Remember that you need feedback in order to improve. Even if your supervisor has not overtly complained about your work, there is usually something that you could have done better, whether in terms of drafting, research or organisation or simply getting other members of staff to assist you.

Some supervisors are not very good at offering this information while you are sitting with them, which of course gives you no opportunity to discuss how you might improve. Try to take a proactive approach and at the end

Experience comparison

One trainee, who thought that she was being taken little account of by being placed with a three year qualified property solicitor found that not only was she working on part of a big land development transaction with him, but that she was also drafting instructions to counsel, doing residential conveyancing, leasing documentation and copious amounts of research – in fact she ended up working for all eight partners in the department while one of her fellow trainees spent his six month seat trailing around checking documents and taking notes for the partner heading up the development project. Who learned most of immediate use?

of any major piece of work in which you are involved with your supervisor, whether it is a piece of conveyancing, setting up a trust, negotiating a share sale and purchase agreement or drafting a statement of case for a mediation, ask for an honest appraisal of how you have performed – and how you could improve.

Make it clear that you are not looking for soft praise but rather a checklist of areas requiring improvement and suggestions as to how you might expedite them. If your supervisor praises your drafting, but comments on some careless errors in marking up documents, don't consider that drafting is a higher order skill and that the missed deletions don't matter. They do. Supervisors expect you to be able to mark up documents flawlessly; the excellent drafting skills are a bonus at this stage.

And don't, whatever you do, let your seat pass without some sort of interim discussions about your good points and your bad points. By the end of the seat it may be too late for you to eradicate your weak points and to enhance your strengths and, worst of all, your supervisor may have submitted a written report emphasising something which it would have been very easy for you to change.

Chapter 5

APPEARANCE MATTERS

SPEED READ SUMMARY

■ People will make snap judgements about your potential competence within a few seconds of meeting you.

■ Looking neat and presentable need not cost a fortune.

■ Dressing appropriately for all occasions, social or business, is important. Make sure that you adhere to some simple sartorial rules.

■ Lawyers are sometimes called to foreign trips at very short notice. Make sure that you are always prepared and ready.

NEAT AND TIDY

There are not too many hard and fast rules about legal dress these days, apart from a requirement that you wear a business suit in court.

Although dark business suits may seem boring, they are like school uniform in that wearing them does save a lot of thought in the morning. And if you do not have a great deal of spare cash they can look smart and last over a period of time without your having to change to suit the vagaries of fashion. The colour black can mask a cheaper material or a less well-cut suit. A brighter impression can be created by the use of a carefully chosen shirt, tie or piece of jewellery.

Many trainees literally 'buy into' the idea that they must have expensive everything to create a good impression. This really is not necessary. One senior associate comments that he and his fellow trainees bought £100 shirts 'because that's what we thought you had to do. As we got more senior and had a lot more money we looked for the four for £100 offers.' The important thing is to look clean, tidy and presentable. Make that part of your personal brand.

UNINTENDED CONSEQUENCES

If you come to work in frayed trousers and a jacket with missing buttons, you'll look lazy and disorganised, your supervisor will be irritated and may well think twice before introducing you to clients. 'I don't know what to do about X,' one partner confided to another, 'he's pretty good, but how can I take him to meetings looking like that? And I don't know what to say, because I don't know whether he can't afford some new shirts or whether he just doesn't care.' (The trainee concerned is now a multi-millionaire entrepreneur – you might not be so lucky.)

SUIT YOUR STATUS

It is often acceptable to remove your jacket in the office and to wear a smart piece of knitwear instead, reserving formality for when you are meeting a client. Remember that clients are paying good money for your advice and want to feel that you are serious enough and prosperous enough to give it. Once you have a reputation as a good lawyer, you can look eccentric and shabby. The Senior Partner with a string of important corporate clients can get away with having a hole in the elbow of his shirt – they'll think that he's just too wrapped up in his clients' business to attend to minor sartorial details.

If you're not sure what the dress code is, ask your supervisor or HR. Whether or not there is a formal written policy, keep your eyes open and watch how other people dress. Whilst you are a trainee, the general rule is to 'fit in'. You don't want to be remarkable for your clothes.

Even if you know nothing, you can at least look as though you can give good advice.

FOR FEMALE TRAINEES...

If you are planning to wear something more colourful and fashionable, think about why you are going to do so. An office is not a night club; it's a workplace. Before you start to dress to reveal your feminine charms think about what you are hoping to achieve and what impression you will give.

Jangly bracelets are irritating for other people and also for you when you are typing or taking notes in a meeting. Very high-heeled shoes can trip you up and add to your tiredness at the end of the day if you are rushing after a fast-walking partner on the way to a meeting. More than likely it will be you who will be carrying a briefcase and several files and not the partner. Pencil skirts that require you to take small steps and slow you down can be a source of annoyance not only to you but to the person having to slow down while you trip along. The partner who is striding ahead eager to get to an urgent court meeting will not thank you that the files she needs are trailing 100 yards behind in your briefcase. Be comfortable and be agile.

Legal offices are full of files, on the desks yes, but also on floors and on shelves which require ladders to reach them. Don't wear short skirts if you don't want people to see your underwear when you bend down or climb a ladder.

You will frequently be looking at the same document or book with the solicitor that you are working for. Don't wear a low-cut top if you do not want to distract others with your cleavage. Check when you buy tops and shirts that they are not see-through – otherwise speculation about the colour of your bra can produce much merriment among the male associates.

In the summer remember that even if it is very warm, you can still look professional. Some offices frown on female staff having bare legs. Just as it's not a good idea to wear a suit on the beach it's not a good idea to wear shorts in a legal office.

Trouser suits are comfortable and non-revealing, and enable you to wear flat shoes without looking frumpy.

Preparation checklist

There is no need to keep a complete wardrobe in the office, but you should at least have the following:
- clean shirt and underwear
- set of toiletries
- collapsible umbrella and a mac or fold-up waterproof
- spare pair of shoes for those days when you arrive at work with wet feet because of torrential rain
- sewing kit for buttons or dropped hems
- shoe-shining sponge

Female trainees should add:
- spare tights or stockings
- pair of black 'heels'
- evening top and some inexpensive jewellery for those days when you are asked with no notice to go to an evening function

FOR MALE TRAINEES...

The options are a bit more limited for male trainees. Although dress codes vary from formal to dress down, you'll notice that in law firms male trainees usually dress in a conservative manner. Formal attire is a dark suit, double-cuffed shirt, low-key tie and black leather shoes. Dress down only usually goes as far as pressed chinos, an open-necked shirt and leather slip-ons. You'll need to go to Bermuda to find lawyers in shorts – and even then they will be tailored and worn with a shirt and tie.

BE PREPARED

The Boy Scout motto should be written in letters of gold in your memory. If you are suddenly asked to attend a client meeting, or help to entertain clients after work, or take the next plane to Athens, or attend a race meeting with a partner (all true examples) then there is not much point in bemoaning the fact that you are inappropriately dressed.

It is also wise to make sure that you are never down to your last 50p just in case you need to take a cab to a client meeting. Don't assume that the partner you are sharing the cab with will have money in his pocket. If he really is busy and successful he may have been too busy to get anywhere near a cash machine that morning and may be relying on you. Unfair? Yes, but remember that you are there to help and to make a good impression and if that means supplying the cab fare, which you can later reclaim from petty cash, then so be it.

Always carry a charged mobile with you when you are out of the office in case the partner you are with asks you to ring the office for some information or to rearrange an appointment. And it might just save your credibility if you yourself need to get some fast advice from the office.

The point here is that the job for the client should not be jeopardised in any way by lack of organisation. It is worthwhile investing in a spare mobile phone charger cable that you can keep at the office – you never know when you might need to recharge your phone, perhaps because you get called away on a business trip at short notice or you have pulled an 'all-nighter'.

PREPARED FOR TAKE-OFF

Before you start your contract buy a small piece of luggage that you can take onboard a plane with you; remember to check airline restrictions on bag dimensions before you buy. International deals require mobile lawyers, who can put a few items of clothing, a small washbag and pile of papers together and literally – go.

Papers are bulky. If you are taking them to a meeting abroad, it's a good idea to get your secretary to arrange double-sided copies on A5 paper. This will take up far less room.

Make sure that you know exactly what the travel arrangements are, down to when you are expected to be at the airport, how much time you will need to get there and allow contingency time for unforeseen leaves on the line or adverse weather conditions. And just like being prepared at

---

Not wanted on voyage

Late one evening a thrilled trainee was asked to accompany two partners on a three-day session in Budapest. He had no time to purchase something more sensible so he threw clothing and papers into the massive suitcase that he had taken to New Zealand during his gap year. The partners, with their cabin friendly luggage, were less than amused when they had to wait at both Budapest and Birmingham airports for the trainee's luggage to come off the carousel.

Another trainee barely survived his supervisor's growing irritation when he turned up at Heathrow with his clean shirt and the deal papers packed into a rather well-used rucksack to go to a set of meetings in New York. As they moved from meeting to meeting, the trainee's fumbling embarrassment grew in proportion to the gradual crumpling of the papers. Remember that the impression that a partner makes on his clients and on other lawyers depends partly on the impression that his trainees convey.

home be prepared abroad – make sure your passport is up-to-date, that your debit or credit cards will work abroad and get some foreign currency for the trip so that, should you need to, you can pay for the cab from the airport or other incidentals and claim them back through expenses on your return. It is not like going on holiday with your parents – the partner is not expecting to have to mother you. Don't stuff up before you start!

Chapter 6

ELEPHANT TRAPS

SPEED READ SUMMARY

- Working in an office is not all about work. This chapter deals with some of the social aspects of working in a legal office.

- Although gossiping is enticing, it can trap you.

- Office relationships are different from college relationships. Be careful that the things you do and say do not affect your long-term prospects.

- The most difficult thing to manage and keep secret in an office is a sexual relationship with a colleague. It's even more difficult with a client.

WHAT ARE ELEPHANT TRAPS?

Tax lawyers often refer to certain situations as 'elephant traps'. You may fall into them unwittingly but the tax consequences can be, just like traps for large animals, very deep indeed in financial terms. 'Elephant trap' is also a good term to describe some of the things in a legal office that may appear innocuous or entirely personal but which may have unforeseen and very unpleasant consequences for your future career.

GOSSIP AND OFFICE POLITICS

Lawyers love gossip, whether it is about their work colleagues, leading counsel or the people that they went to university or college with. You can pick up valuable pieces of information from pre- and post-meeting discussions between your supervisor and other lawyers.

But beware. Supervisors also want to know what is going on in the office and some see their trainees as valuable sources of information. They may shamelessly pump you about who is going out with whom, who is related to whom, what X does in his spare time, what Y is working on now, what it's like to work with Z. While it is all very flattering to be part of a conversation with a more senior member of the firm, ask yourself why they are so interested in what you have to say.

They may simply be passing the time with lightweight conversation, but you do not want to get a reputation for passing on titbits about or, worse still, bad-mouthing your fellow trainees; they are your peer group after all. And be careful not to be seen to be taking sides in some feud between senior colleagues that you only gradually become aware of. Just because people work in a partnership does not mean that they actually like each other; there may be years of resentment and antipathy between two people in an office. If you can avoid it do not get yourself into a situation where you are being pumped by one of them for information about the other. If they are doing this the chances are that your colleagues are also being pumped for information about you.

GOSSIP'S GOLDEN RULE

Until you are absolutely certain you understand the politics of the firm (and who holds power and who is allied to whom) which can often take years, keep your eyes and your ears open and your lips firmly shut when it comes to gossip. As one wise person said, 'God gave you two ears, two eyes and one mouth. Use them in that proportion.'

SLEEPING WITH THE ENEMY

The law firm village is a whole new territory as far as personal relationships are concerned. Unfortunately working long hours means that you often have no chance of meeting someone you might fancy other than your work colleagues or your clients. You can literally get into the office in the morning, spend all day in your room apart from trips to the coffee machine or the sandwich bar and then go home again at night too brain dead to do anything other than slump in front of the television.

You will often find yourself socialising with your colleagues because that is the easy thing to do. Some firms definitely encourage this by providing sports facilities and restaurants and organised trips. You will probably find that many of the partners have long-term friendships with other partners which began when they were trainees, or rather articled clerks. A law firm can be a very tight-knit village indeed.

FRIENDSHIP BUT NOT SEX

The big problem with sexual relationships is that most of them break up. Although managing an office relationship can be difficult, this is as nothing to the potential difficulties where such a relationship does not survive.

The one thing that you can be sure of, whatever the size of your firm, is that there will be no permanent anonymity. The mere hint of a glance across a crowded room and someone will be scanning the holiday lists to see if you have both booked time out at the same time; it will certainly be noted if you share a taxi home after a casual departmental trip to the pub round the corner.

While all is going well you will be able to cope with the teasing and might even enjoy it, but if the relationship breaks up, remember that this is not university where you can duck a few classes or take a few days off for emergency recuperation. Most universities are big enough to let you avoid the other person; law firms are not. Universities also have eight to ten week terms after which you can go home to lick your wounds. In a law firm you are there all year except for your possibly meagre annual leave.You will just have to get up the next day and get on with your job in the full public glare of your misery.

DIFFERENTIAL FALLOUT

Gone are the days when there were very strict rules about intra-office relationships and when it was almost a sacking offence for a male trainee to go out with a secretary. Now it is not impossible for partners in even the largest firms to be married to each other. Until her term of office was up, the Managing Partner of one of the major City firms was a woman married to another partner. In a smaller firm having a husband and wife who are both partners can produce tensions for the other partners. After all, the spat that started over the cornflakes can easily drift into a partnership meeting later in the day.

Trainees having relationships with their office colleagues put themselves in potentially difficult positions if the relationship founders. Breaking up with another trainee produces awkwardness and teasing comments. If you decide to run the gauntlet of an office romance be prepared to take the consequences and check that you don't fall foul of the firm's policy. You may be required to declare formally your 'affiliation'.

CRUSHES ON YOUR SUPERVISOR

It is not uncommon for trainees to develop crushes on their supervisors and vice versa. After all you may spend hours working together, having intellectually stimulating conversations, getting to know each other personally, sharing the excitement of closing a deal or winning a case. It can be heady stuff. But even if the feeling appears mutual, the golden rule is to keep the relationship on a professional level.

If you are ditched, you will, for at least some time to come, be sharing an office with the person who has hurt you. Perhaps more important than your own personal misery, remember that supervisors are in a position to do serious damage to your career if you slight them. And also remember that the more senior the person concerned, then the more damage that can be done.

Even if the partner that you have upset takes the broken relationship in a mature way, there may still be an embarrassment factor in your relationship with other partners. Will they feel comfortable praising your work in front of the slighted partner? Or even give you a fair assessment? Will they recommend that you be kept on if it will produce awkwardness? To make matters worse your supervisor or the senior solicitor concerned may be breaching disciplinary codes. At best, others will question their judgement and whether they abused their power over you.

While you are a trainee you are very vulnerable to the effects of relationships gone wrong, particularly if the person with whom you have the relationship, even if not a partner, has any power to affect your future career or your annual report.

THE ULTIMATE TABOO

The most potentially hazardous relationship in which you can indulge is one with a client.

This jeopardises professional distance and puts you in a difficult position with your colleagues, because you are making it difficult for them to know whether they should treat you as a junior colleague or as the partner of the client. This is a dangerous position for you to be in, especially if the relationship breaks up.

Think about the following:
■ How will your supervisor feel about taking you to meetings involving that particular client or the organisation that he works for? He may very well not think that your intimate knowledge of the client is an advantage to the firm. He may find the relationship just plain embarrassing.
■ If you ditch the client, and the client has sufficient business to give the firm, then the firm may 'realise' that it will lose his work if it does not dispense with your services. Looking at it objectively, if you were a Managing Partner, would you choose a client who can give the firm £200,000 of business in a year over a trainee who probably will not turn out to be the best lawyer in the world anyway? Would your supervisor be likely to jeopardise the relationship with a local family who have been with the firm for 40 years because you have fallen out with a member of it?
■ On the other hand, if the client ditches you, then you may well have to hide your upset and humiliation in future meetings. Feeling that it might enhance the relationship with the client, your supervisor will now be in a position to take out on you any previous feelings of envy or irritation at your previous behaviour. How sympathetic are your colleagues likely to be to your predicament? If they work for this client, you could be putting them in a position where their loyalties are divided.

One thing is certain, your hurt and humiliation could be very public, and possibly not confined to your law firm.

SECRET TRYSTS

You may think that you can keep the relationship, whether with a fellow trainee, a senior colleague or more dangerously with a client, secret from everyone, and this may be possible in the short term. It may even give you a buzz. But think about it. Are you really prepared to put your career on the line for a relationship that is probably temporary? Is it really worth messing up your concentration and diluting your dedication to your future career? You've worked hard to get where you are now. This is the time to follow your head and not your heart.

Chapter 7

'POUR THE COFFEE, DARLING' – HOW TO MANAGE COMMON OFFICE SITUATIONS

SPEED READ SUMMARY

■ Everyone needs sustenance during a meeting. Don't take offence if you are asked to organise it. Take charge of the situation and make it work for you.

■ Considering the needs of others will demonstrate not just fellow feeling, but also your ability to plan ahead.

■ Don't get mad about photocopying. Just get it right.

COFFEE SOCIOLOGY

Being asked to pour the coffee (or make the tea for that matter) is not exactly an invitation to leap headlong into an elephant trap, but it is a good example of how a relatively trivial thing can assume an unnecessary symbolic importance in an office context. It is one of those little things that irritate women at all levels and men at the more junior level. However, before you become irate about being asked to perform what may seem to you to be a menial task, analyse the underlying reasoning behind your being asked. If you don't like the result, then think calmly about how you are going to deal with future requests.

In many offices there is still an assumption that if there is a woman in the room at a meeting she will pour the coffee, and if not, that the most junior man will do so. It is very easy to get hung up about this and to spend time worrying about it and analysing what it says about other people's perceptions of you.

The bottom line is that someone has got to do it, so stand back and look at it objectively.

REASONS WHY YOU MAY BE ASKED TO POUR THE COFFEE:

- The partner you are with is deep in negotiation with the other side. Asking you to pour the coffee buys a bit of thinking time.
- Your partner is simply bored with looking at these papers and would like a bit of ocular relaxation.
- Your partner thinks that you are less likely to spill the stuff than anyone else present.
- He genuinely thinks that a woman, any woman, can do this better than any man.

There are many reasons for asking you to pour the coffee other than wishing to demean you. Although do not discount that as a reason either.

SO WHAT DO YOU DO ABOUT IT?

Outside the meeting ask the partner concerned whether there is an office rule dealing with refreshments. Do this in a genuinely enquiring and not in a complaining tone. You might receive one or several of the following answers:

The most junior person present pours the coffee. This is helpful because you know that you should be able to delegate that role as soon as you qualify, if not sooner.

The person who is 'not doing anything' at the meeting pours the coffee. One partner never asked the trainee that he took to meetings to pour the coffee because that trainee's function was to take notes and to observe the facial nuances of the lawyers on the other side. This is fairly comforting at the most junior level, but means that you will probably be pouring coffee for the trainees when you yourself are qualified. But, learn a little humility. As you will have realised by then, it's difficult enough for trainees to feel valued.

The person nearest the coffee pours the coffee. This is easy. If you don't want to pour, just don't sit anywhere near the coffee if you can help it, but you will have to accept that this may sometimes conflict with being in the seat at the meeting that you would prefer.

The most junior woman at the meeting pours the coffee. This would probably be said jocularly if at all, but it is implicit in many unspoken and often unconscious assumptions about women's role in the workplace. You could be outraged, but it's perhaps more effective to smile and ask 'Why?' If you get the response that men don't know how to do it properly, then suggest that HR or Marketing should lay on a lunch-time course to show them how to do it. 'After all, there are not always women present at meetings. What do you do then?'

The female trainees pour the coffee. This is truly unacceptable, because it suggests that in meetings where there are both male and female trainees, the female trainees will always wait on the male ones. You may actively have to say, 'It's your turn this time, James' to a male trainee at a meeting, but then be prepared for him to remind you that it is yours on the next occasion.

POURING THE COFFEE CAN BE SENSIBLE IF...

- You want to stretch your legs
- The colleague you are with is elderly, or disabled, or has broken a leg skiing
- You are part of the discussion and you want time to think
- You know that the partner you are with is not going to look after the client properly, corralling the milk and sugar at the end of the table farthest from the client and then absent-mindedly munching through all the biscuits

without offering them to the client. This is a judgement call, and you have to ask yourself what is more important, the client or your pride?

IF YOU DO POUR THE COFFEE:

Serve the clients first. And all of them. But remember that it is 'ladies first' – this isn't double standards but is simply what is polite expectation. Then serve the most senior person on your side and then go round the table. If you later feel that clients are looking for biscuits and they are on the other side of the table AND you are not doing something else, then get up and reposition them.

If there are no clients, then serve the most senior 'guest' lawyer on the other side first (remember that you might be looking for a job at that firm one day) and then go round the table. Offer the milk, sugar and biscuits first, then leave them on the table by the most senior colleague on your side. It is then up to your colleague to demonstrate good manners or otherwise by passing them round.

But don't be subservient. There is no need to keep bobbing up and down to attend to the other people present. There is no need to walk round the room handing milk, sugar and biscuits to everyone individually – unless they are clients. However, if you are getting the feeling that you are about to be asked to pour a second round for people, it's a good idea to offer. Try to take control of the situation. You'll feel a whole lot better.

Do use your common sense. You are a mature and professional human being, who is treating other human beings with courtesy, so smile if you are going to do it rather than be churlish. You can talk about it after the meeting if necessary.

AND ANOTHER THING...

It can be very tempting to pocket leftover chocolate biscuits at the end of a meeting, but you should remember:
- Don't take them from other firms' offices.
- Don't remove them while clients or lawyers from another firm are there. That just looks cheap.
- Don't take a handful, especially if a partner is present. It just looks greedy. Although you shouldn't be stocking up for the rest of the week, no one minds if you take one or two for a tea break later in the day. Don't abuse this hospitality or take it for granted.

FORWARD PLANNING

Forward planning isn't just about diarising court dates and filing dates. It also means thinking about other people and what is the best way for all of you to operate. If you know or suspect that it is going to be a long meeting, ask the partner concerned whether you should organise sandwiches and snacks. Find out what the likely lunch or evening meal plans are and quietly check people's dietary requirements. Having the telephone numbers of takeaway and food delivery services to hand will indicate that you are organised and proactive. Being mindful of the physical needs of others is not weak, it is actually efficient.

TO PHOTOCOPY OR NOT TO PHOTOCOPY?

This is another one of those things, like pouring the coffee, that trainees (and even partners) can get fairly worked up about. Not so long ago one partner gave as the reason for not wanting to take on older trainees that they would be expected to do photocopying and that this would be demeaning for an older person.

The best advice here is not to take an unnecessary stand about it. There will be times when documents need to be copied for clients and no secretaries or support staff are available. Accept with a good grace that it is your role in such circumstances. It is not a good idea to stand by and watch your senior colleagues struggling to get a court bundle or other urgent documents copied. Even if it is eleven pm, now is not the time to get your coat. However dog-tired you may be, offer to take over or help out. A gesture such as this is probably going to count more than 50 pieces of legal research when it comes to your appraisal, because it shows that you are a 'team player'.

However, it is perfectly permissible at other times to indicate to your supervisor that you are giving the photocopying to someone else. If challenged, the appropriate response is not 'This is not what you are paying me for, is it?' (actually they are paying you to do more or less anything that they can think of at the time) but 'Wouldn't you prefer that I did your research note first? You said that you needed it by four pm.'

If your supervisor really does want you to do the photocopying for some complicated reason that isn't clear to you, then there can hardly be a complaint afterwards if the work needed by four pm is not done by then. It's possible that your supervisor gets a power kick out of making you do the photocopying but sometimes your supervisor will genuinely need the photocopying to be done by you and only you. For example, court bundles wrongly put together can be a source of extreme annoyance to judges and badly photocopied bundles have been the cause of angry explosions from the High Court bench.

THE MECHANICS OF PHOTOCOPYING

A word or two of advice about the mechanics of photocopying: learn about the special features of the photocopier which often include collating, hole-punching, stapling etc. If a photocopying lesson forms part of the induction process in your firm, take it seriously, as familiarity with the different forms of photocopier available can save you an enormous amount of time when you are under pressure.

Watch out for the most frequent human photocopying error (particularly easy to do if you are tired or in a rush) – copying a set of papers in the usual way without noticing that the originals are in fact double-sided. You will have to start all over again but this could be the least of your worries – sometimes the mistake has only been discovered later by a partner under pressure who has been understandably irate.

So, if you are the only person that your supervisor can rely on to do the photocopying, don't waste energy in getting annoyed; concentrate and get it right first time!

Chapter 8

PRESENTING YOUR WORK

SPEED READ SUMMARY

- Legal work is often presented in written form, and the client expects you to get it right.

- Make sure that you take down instructions accurately and agree a deadline for completion of your work.

- Analyse the problem you have been given, decide what additional information you require and carry out the necessary research.

- Tailor your response to your audience, recognising that the format and tone will be different if you are writing letters to clients, general notes, Instructions to Counsel or notes for partners.

- Every firm has its own way of setting out letters. Make sure you get the format and the form of address correct.

- Completing a piece of work is often about presenting it to the person who asked for it as much as about answering the actual question. Supervisors may not always get the answer they want; you need to learn how to deliver bad news.

The presentation mantra:
- **Listen**
- **Write**
- **Analyse**
- **Research**
- **Write**
- **Present**

BEFORE YOU START

Legal work is on the whole written work and to some extent every time that you produce a piece of written work you are sitting an examination. This will not change in the whole of your legal career. Every time that you write a letter of advice for a client you are testing yourself to get it right, to find the right solution for that particular client, so that she can get a better deal in a commercial venture, so that he can get off a driving offence, so that she can negotiate a lesser tax penalty with HM Revenue and Customs, or so that he can persuade his neighbours to cut down the tree that is overhanging his garden.

The difference from all the thinking and writing that you have done before is that this is real, and the only acceptable pass mark is 100%. If the advice is bad or your drafting is shoddy then at the very least the client will not come back and at the worst you can be sued. Solicitors reckon that they are very fortunate indeed if they are not sued more than once in their professional careers. That is why the premiums on professional indemnity insurance are so high. And if you're the cause of a suit against the firm, you won't be thanked for the resulting hike in insurance premiums the following year.

This has an effect on how you should view the work that you are given to do. Sometimes if they are not too pressed your supervising solicitors will give you work which is designed to extend your knowledge and skills although it may have little relevance to the work that they themselves are carrying out. But usually you will be given something to do because your supervisor has need of it – because he or she is under pressure.

So you must do your best to get it right. It may seem trivial or on the other hand totally above your head, but remember that it is being given to you because a client needs it.

HELP YOUR SUPERVISOR

There is no point in spending several hours on something if you do not know what you are doing. When you sit exams the only person who is hurt if you misunderstand a question is you, but in the work situation you can hurt other people as well, and this will not necessarily be forgotten or understood. One of the most difficult things for trainees to understand after 20 years of solid education is that the people who are there supposedly to help them do not view that as their primary purpose at all.

Don't pretend you know all about something when you don't. The chances are that you will be found out. But don't volunteer your total ignorance either. You can usually find out the answer.

TAKING INSTRUCTIONS

Your supervisors will probably give you something to do when they are under pressure, often when they have just returned from a meeting with a client or another partner. You may well not have their undivided attention when you are being given instructions, the telephone may ring halfway through or someone else may come into the office. There are a hundred different reasons why instructions may be rushed.

In addition some solicitors are just plain bad at giving instructions. This is often true of solicitors who are regarded as 'brilliant' by other people in the office. What they may want you to research is some tiny point of law. In their own minds they have whittled the problem down to this one tiny point, but they forget to give you the context. And, as they say, context is all...

ALWAYS WRITE DOWN INSTRUCTIONS

On the other hand you may have been given perfect instructions which are clear and concise, but unfortunately just as your supervisor has finished instructing you, your phone rings or someone else comes into the office to ask you to do something urgently. An hour later you do not recollect what you have been asked to do and your supervisor is now out at a meeting. The only thing that you do remember is that the work is required by nine am the following day.

Even if you have a phenomenal memory and can rely on it, don't. When you are asked to go to someone else's office, even if you think you know what it is about, take a notebook with you. Far from demonstrating to a partner that your memory is above reproach, not taking notes suggests either arrogance or a casual attitude to work. You might be caught by another partner on the way back to your office and may not be able to sit down and think about the assigned task for an hour or more, when you will have forgotten a very high proportion of what you have been told. (If you need proof of the evanescence of short-term memory, then ask a friend to participate in the short experiment at the end of this chapter.)

Watch experienced solicitors when they talk to clients on the phone. Most of them will be jotting down information as they converse with the client. If you get the chance watch how the good note-takers have developed their own shorthand. Adopt useful abbreviations and develop your own. Good note-takers will often have smaller and smoother handwriting (because it's quicker) and they will be selective in what they write.

If you make a habit of writing things down, then even if your instructions have been inadequate, you will be able to use your notes to point out (tactfully) what you understood your supervisor to mean.

SET A DATE

Always ask for a deadline. If you are told 'by four pm on Friday' that will help you when your supervisor asks at three pm on Wednesday why you haven't prepared a draft yet. You can hardly ask your supervisor to sign your notebook in agreement to a time, but it is a good idea to write it down carefully at the end of your noted instructions so that the supervisor can see it.

If you know that it is going to be impossible for you to complete the work on time, then say so. Explain why (I already have this research on boundaries to do for X and this sub-lease to do for Y) and ask your supervisor which you should prioritise. It may be that it would be acceptable for it to be done by a later date. It may be possible for the supervisor to find someone else to do it instead. At least give your supervisor, however gruff, a choice. At the time there may be muttering and frowning, but that will be as nothing to the muttering and frowning that there will be if you agree to complete a task by a certain date and you are unable to deliver.

PUBLIC REMINDER

A prominent display of the work you are engaged in is a reminder of your deadline for completion and an indication to other people of just how busy you are.

If you have a whiteboard in your office use it to demonstrate your commitments. List:
- a brief description of each individual piece of work
- who it is for
- the matter number
- the date it is due

If no whiteboard is available, then an updated sheet of paper on your desk will suffice, although it does not make such a persuasive statement.

BEFORE YOU START WORK

The last thing that you should do is to start work on something before you understand what you are being asked to do. You will not only waste your own time, you will also waste your supervisor's if he has to read a ten-page dissertation on joint tenancies in the hope that the point he wanted to know about on tenancies in common is in there somewhere.

If you don't understand what you are being asked to do, it is perfectly sensible to say that you don't quite understand a particular point, or to ask if your supervisor would not mind going over something again. But don't ask three times in a row.

You have to use some common sense here, because some people resent having to repeat themselves, or may simply be in a hurry. You will also find that there are some people whose instructions are so bad that you will always have to go away and work out what they are REALLY asking you to do, so that you can return with some properly formulated questions.

'What you are asking me to do is... '

It's often quite wise to test that you really have understood your instructions by summarising your instructions to your supervisor. When he says 'Do you understand that?' don't nod blindly, summarise if you can. If you really are in a fog, go away and think about it and then come back to check.

'I've been looking at this again, and I'd just like to check that I've got the detail absolutely right before I start work.'

In contrast to all of the people who have been teaching you over the past 20 years it will be very unusual if your supervisor has been trained to teach. That is not how she makes a living. She is, just as you are, making it up as she goes along. Some people are very good at this, and some are not. It's up to you to take the most that you can out of the situation.

SETTING ABOUT THE TASK

You are back at your desk with your notes. Now what do you do?

What you might have been asked to do can vary from the extremely complex and time-consuming to the very simple. You could be asked to prepare a note on a topic, find a point of law, draft a contractual provision, write a will, solve a simple tax problem, advise on evidence or draft a defence. All of these things are in the nature of a solicitor's job.

Numerous books have been written on how you search for legal material and in a larger firm your library may well have some. It's a good idea to familiarise yourself very quickly with the location of the books and journals used by the department in which you are sitting. Having a precise idea of where they are located and a rough idea of what is in them will be very helpful. Supervisors often think that they know where something is, but none of us is perfect, so be prepared to search to find what you have been asked to locate. (Also see Chapter 10.)

PRACTICAL RESEARCH PRESENTATION

It is possible that someone else may already have researched the point that you have been asked to consider (or something similar) and written it up, so as a first step search your firm's know-how database if it has one, email other trainees in the department, but don't get a reputation as someone who is regularly sending global emails asking for help. Don't be afraid to use online legal resources (Lawtel, PLC, Westlaw for example) or to Google it. Although the answers you receive will most likely not be sufficient in themselves to answer your question, a few minutes spent at the computer should give you some useful pointers.

Remember that pointers are exactly that, an indication of what the answers might be; always check the legal position by consulting the primary source, whether legislation or case law, since the position may have changed since the previous research was carried out. If you rely on the work of a colleague, remember to acknowledge the source; you will certainly annoy your colleagues if you deliberately or inadvertently pass their work off as your own.

If you have been asked to research a specific point, then once you have found the relevant information read it, try to understand it, take a few minutes to ascertain whether you need more information in order to understand it, then summarise it in your own words either in writing if you have time, or in your head going back to your desk, so that you can explain it to your supervisor. That is your training.

To help your supervisor it is a good idea to photocopy any page or pages where the point was explained, highlighting the relevant sections. This can then be placed in the appropriate file. In six months' time you will have moved on to another department, but the file will remain. If you merely give an oral report, then the research is in effect lost.

When your research is completed, and if the point is new or is an update of previous guidance, ask your supervisor whether you should send a short email to the rest of the group. This gets you the maximum benefit from your work as it is a good way to raise your profile.

THE WIDER CONTEXT

If you have been asked to look at a specific problem that will require more detailed research or lengthier consideration, do not immediately home in on a word that is unfamiliar or on a case that your supervisor has mentioned briefly. Try to ascertain from what has been said why you are being asked to look at something. Who is the client? What does the client want?

Think around the problem. For example, if you are asked to draft a will for a man with a wife and three children, it is very easy to think only about saving tax. You might consider including a provision for what is called a 'nil rate band discretionary trust' in favour of the children; this will operate to place that portion of the testator's estate after death which is under the threshold where inheritance tax becomes payable (£312,000 for the tax year 2008–2009, but it goes up annually) in trust for his children. The remainder of the estate may then be left to his wife if she survives him.

The idea behind this is that the amount that will be capable of being left Inheritance Tax free in the nil rate band trust will always be the maximum amount permitted by law. No Inheritance Tax will be payable on the wife's remainder because she will benefit from spouse exemption, so that the net result will be that no Inheritance Tax will be paid on the husband's estate when he dies.

But what if the husband's estate is relatively modest? There is not much point in saving Inheritance Tax on an estate of £500,000 if the widow is left with only £188,000. That may seem like a lot of money to you, but may not get the widow very far, when it has to take care of her for the rest of her life. If the house in which she is living at her husband's death forms part of her husband's estate it may also have to be sold to put the trust in funds.

Remember that the essence of being a good solicitor is to put yourself in the shoes of your clients and to think what is best for them in the long, as well as the short, run.

SETTING OUT YOUR ANSWERS

Most of the time your supervisor will not want an academic dissertation. Sometimes, for example if he is drafting complicated instructions to counsel, that is exactly what is required. But at other times, although you may have to do a fair amount of reading, all that is wanted is a snappy little letter to a client explaining that the responsibility for maintaining a mutual boundary fence is hers and not her neighbour's.

If you can, try to find out what is the ultimate purpose of what you are being asked to do before you start work. This can be tricky because some partners are so absorbed in what they are doing that they can either assume that you know all the background as well, or equally fatally, consider that it is simply not necessary for you to know what they are going to do with the result of your endeavours. But it can make a big difference to your presentation if you know how your work might ultimately be used.

DOING A RESEARCH NOTE

There could be many different reasons for your supervisor asking you to do a research note on a topic or point of law, such as your supervisor:
- Feels that what he is being asked to advise on turns on a nice point of law
- Knows that a new case may have a bearing on general advice she is giving, but she does not have time at the moment to read both it and the learned commentaries that have been written on it
- Has been asked to give an opinion to a member of another department
- Is writing Instructions to Counsel and needs to have some precise detail
- Is writing a letter to a client
- Is writing an article for a journal

There are many different reasons and it is sensible to find out, if you can, why you are being asked to carry out the research because that may affect the way that you write it up. If the research is for a client letter you may, if you have the time, try your hand at expressing complex law in simple language while at the same time presenting a more formal exegesis.

Whatever the end purpose there are some basic rules to follow in writing up most pieces of research:

- The first paragraph should contain a short summary of the facts and the gist of what you have been asked to do. If you can't do this, then go no further, because you will most likely be carrying out an 'all I know about x' exercise, instead of focusing on the point at issue. A summary also gives your supervisor a quick opportunity to check that you have really understood what you have been asked to do, instead of having to wade through five pages of dense prose to discover that you were off on a frolic of your own.
- Next set out your research, with paragraph headings and sub-headings to make it easier for your supervisor to follow the thread of your investigation.
- Make sure that you cite all references properly, so that someone else can check them if necessary.
- Finally, come to a conclusion if possible, referring back to the first paragraph and give reasons. This is a useful check that you have actually carried out the research you were assigned.

The way in which you present your results should in addition be informed by the purposes for which it is to be used.

LETTERS TO CLIENTS

In most firms you will not be permitted to write even the simplest letter to a client or to anyone else without it being checked by your supervisor. It may be some time before you are permitted to send out a letter under your own name. Most of the time you will be writing as from your supervisor or more formally in the name of your firm. Once again this is a simple insurance precaution.

However, you can be of great assistance to your supervisors if you consider why they are writing the letters in the first place and consider the appropriate presentation of the information that you have been asked for.

Your supervisor may be writing to a client who is a private individual. Ideally your supervisor would prefer to be able to 'drop in' part of your answer into the letter with only a few tweaks to make it more personal.

In the first paragraph set out what the issue is, but you could make it more personal – 'you asked me whether... '

Try to put your analysis and conclusions into plain English. This is a good test of how well you have understood the results of your research and should also make it easier for your supervisor to get his letter off quickly. If you have time also attach a more detailed analysis with case and legislative references so that the partner can check your reasoning and sources. You should always be able to identify your sources. It is no good saying, 'the answer is X because I read it somewhere'. Your conclusion must have a legal basis and you must know what that is.

In any event keep a note of your reasoning, however scrappy, for future reference and just in case of the worst case scenario where your firm is sued for its advice. Although every case is slightly different on its facts, many are concerned with similar issues and it is experience and the ability to evaluate and use that experience that makes a good lawyer.

Your supervisor may be writing to an individual client who is also a professional such as another solicitor or an accountant, who will want to have a more meaty reply to his query. In this case you need not make such an effort to write in plain English as a more technical response is what is required.

Your supervisor may be writing to the Chief Executive of a large plc. To some extent the amount of time that you can spend on a piece of research will depend on the type of client who is paying. Large companies have deeper pockets to pay for legal advice and documentation and getting it wrong can be vastly expensive not only for them but for your firm. On the other hand some well-thought-out advice can improve a company's negotiating position and therefore save it substantial sums.

One very large firm sometimes sent senior corporate clients a three-part advice package. First a one-page letter from a senior partner, summarising the question that the client asked followed by a succinct single paragraph of advice, second a two- to three-page summary of the research that was carried out by a more junior colleague and then the full-blown 20-page research note itself. The client could read only the first letter if he chose, but he was also able to see the effort that had gone into providing that brief paragraph of essential advice in the one-page letter.

However, do not skimp on research done for a small private client; getting this wrong can cause irritation and more...

BASIC ADVICE LETTER STRUCTURE

Try setting out your work using this basic structure; it can help you clarify things in your own mind and can be a useful means to get you started when your mind feels as blank as the page in front of you.

- Issues – the question/s you are asked to address
- The facts
- The relevant law
- How the law applies to the facts
- Your conclusions and recommendations

Some clients merely want a list of dos and don'ts, and fairly simple instructions, but you need to have a very sophisticated grasp of the law and a real understanding of the issues and the individual client's position in order to be able to do this successfully.

GETTING YOUR LETTERS RIGHT

This may seem obvious, but it is important to follow the firm's style in the matter of layout and method of addressing clients.

Names of clients and correct form of address. Even if a partner is asking you to do something as simple as sending an acknowledgment letter to 'Mrs Smith', check that she really is Mrs Smith and not Mrs Smyth or Miss Smith. You can check the name of a corporate client easily on the internet, and this is worth doing because companies can adopt strange spellings of common words simply for effect.

If you are drafting a letter from your supervisor to the client, check in the file to see how that client is addressed. 'Dear Mrs Bloggs', 'Dear Candida' or 'Dear Lady Bloggs'. It saves your supervisor time in amending your letter – he will find plenty of other things to amend – and it shows that you are paying attention to detail.

If you are writing a letter from yourself to a client, then address the client formally until you are sure that it would be appropriate to do otherwise, especially if the client is much older than you. 'Dear Mrs Bloggs' rather than 'Dear Candida' is always the safer option.

In a Private Client department modes of addressing people are a minefield, and sometimes your supervisor will not know. Find out which secretary has a copy of *Debrett's Correct Form* or where in the library it can be located. This will save you a great deal of time when you are suddenly asked how the daughter of a Marchioness should be addressed. (The answer is Dear Lady Candida.) An up-to-date copy of *Who's Who* may also help you to ascertain the correct way to address your client.

If you are sending papers to counsel, check whether counsel is a QC or not; some are very touchy about this. Don't take a blanket approach and append the suffix QC to all names. This would not go down well with a barrister who has just been refused for the third time.

REFERENCES AND WHAT THEY MEAN

Firms use references as an indication of the various people involved in the production of a letter. Some firms use numbers which are allocated to individuals as soon as they join the firm; this can therefore enable you to assess how long someone has been with a particular firm. Others use the initials of the fee-earners concerned. Some add the number or initials of the secretary who typed the letter.

51/478/1066 could be the responsible partner (51), the assistant delegated (478) and the trainee who actually wrote the letter (1066).

MST/JLS/RG could be the responsible partner (MST), the trainee who wrote the letter (JLS) and the secretary who typed it (RG).

When you are writing a letter don't skip this part. Not putting your firm's references on the letter will irritate your supervisor. Putting them in the correct place will help those dealing with the matter subsequently to identify who was involved with it at that particular time and also where to find the saved document on the computer system.

You should also copy the reference of the firm to whom you are responding into the appropriate place on your letter. Not to do so is thoughtless. Personnel in other firms can change. If the letter addressed to 'Mr Brown' at a firm with several hundred lawyers also has a complete reference it will be much easier for the other side to identify the appropriate person to deal with your letter if Mr Brown has left the firm. Otherwise your letter could languish in a purgatory of letters for which no one takes responsibility.

Worst of all is the short letter acknowledging the contents of a letter received from another firm which is addressed 'Dear Sir' and signed with the name of the sending firm, which has no references to aid identification. The first time that you are handed such a letter and asked to find out which fee-earner in your firm (perhaps with 100 fee-earners or more) this should go to, you will realise not only how irritating this is, but what a criminal waste of time it all is.

DATES

Dates on letters are important identifiers.

When you have taken so much time and trouble getting everything else correct, don't spoil it by forgetting to insert the correct date. Partners and supervisors will be irritated if they read a reply from a client that starts 'Thank you for your undated letter.' (It can be equally embarrassing if an old template has been used and the old date has been left on the new letter.)

When replying to a letter always identify which letter you are responding to with a simple formula such as 'Thank you for your letter dated 1st May 2008.' This will ensure that it is clear on the file exactly what has been said in response to what. It will then be relatively easy to create a paper trail for the preparation of trial bundles.

LETTER FORMALITIES

'Dear Sir' or 'Dear Madam' and 'Yours faithfully' go together.

A letter addressed to a named person such as 'Dear Mrs Bloggs' or 'Dear Candida' should end 'Yours sincerely'. If you feel that you have got to know the client or the solicitor on the other side reasonably well, then you might add 'Kind regards' before the 'Yours sincerely'.

It saves time if you have worked out some acceptable beginnings to letters. 'As promised I enclose... ' or 'I've now had an opportunity to consider' or 'When you came in last Wednesday you asked me to advise you on... '

Avoid clichéd endings if at all possible. For instance, 'If I can assist you further, please do not hesitate to get in contact' is so uninspiring that it is virtually meaningless and sounds like you couldn't be bothered to finish off the letter with anything original.

INSTRUCTIONS TO COUNSEL

You will probably have learned a general format for these on the LPC. In addition most firms have precedents, but don't slavishly follow precedents. The important thing is that counsel gets properly instructed.

Small instructions will be confined to setting out the facts and asking counsel to opine or to draft another document. The larger instructions will take time. There may be hundreds or even thousands of pages to copy. Take care with every one. You never know which piece of paper may contain that killer piece of evidence. Drafting instructions can take a lot of time, as doing the research before you begin to draft may in itself take many hours.

In all cases it is important that all the facts relevant to the client's position are set out concisely and accurately. This will assist counsel, familiarise you with nuances and in the end save costs for the client. Take as much care with Instructions to Counsel as you would with any other piece of work, because as you yourself will appreciate one day, solicitors hate being found out in spelling mistakes or legal inaccuracies by barristers.

It is a good idea to ask your supervisor or someone else in your current department if they can let you see Instructions to Counsel prepared for another matter or client so that you can see what the preferred style for that department is.

Counsel's advice is often akin to an insurance policy; if your client has £25 million at stake then £10,000 for a second opinion is cheap at twice the price and reassuring for the solicitor. But counsel's opinion must be based on accurate instructions. Take care.

YOUR OWN PERSONAL RESEARCH RESOURCE

Keep a precedents folder of research you have undertaken and documents you have drafted. If you are asked to do something similar again, you will have a place to start without having to look for a file which may well be being worked on by someone else at the time.

Take a little time to consider how you will file this to make the items easy to retrieve. A simple indexing system that files under name of client, name of fee-earner you did the work for and nature of research, advice or document should enable you to identify quickly the answer to such requests as:

- What did you write to that Frenchwoman two months ago about bringing money into the country?
- You drafted an amended dilapidations clause for Rogue Property Rentals, didn't you? We didn't use it at the time but I need it in half an hour.

IF YOU ARE STUCK...

Always remember that you have been given a piece of work for a reason, which is ultimately related to getting advice to the client and hence money for the firm. If you don't understand what you have been asked to do, or you have got so far with your research and can get no further, then look for help. But don't leave it until the last minute. 'I'm sorry, I couldn't do it,' is not an adequate excuse to the partner standing over you looking for the first draft of a will when the client is due in half an hour. There are degrees of wrath; the temperature goes up the nearer it is to a deadline when things go wrong. You may as well get it over with as soon as possible.

Remember also that as in many situations there are people who can help you. (See Chapter 10.) Often they are very close at hand. If, for example, you have been asked to draft a new document ask your supervisor or the previous trainee (who is in any case usually a good source of information) whether there are any useful examples or precedents.

DON'T SHOOT THE MESSENGER

Some people are simply unable to cope with 'bad news'. If a partner has given an off-the-cuff piece of advice to a client, has doubts about it and asks you to research it, he could learn that the advice he gave was inaccurate. He may be grateful that he now knows the correct answer, but then he may not. At that particular juncture there is only one person that he can easily take it out on. You. This is usually a good point to find some urgent work to do that will take you out of the room.

If you sense that the answer that you are going to give is not going to be to your supervisor's liking, you could adopt the strategy of writing a very careful note 'that I thought that you would like for the file'. You will still probably be quizzed about it, but it will avoid the constant interrupting and badgering that some people indulge in when they are listening to information that they do not like. Using this in conjunction with the 'urgent work somewhere else in the office' ploy may just help you to escape the worst of the misdirected wrath.

In this category of 'bad news' may come your supervisor's sheer disbelief that another department does not have the same impeccable record-keeping protocols as your supervisor imagines that she has. One poor trainee was sent six times over the course of a month from one department to another on a fruitless search for a copy of a signed document. It was the practice of the second department to send out final documents to the client but it was not in the nature of the work done for the client that a copy of the signed document was returned to the solicitors. The first department on the other hand was engaged in tax arrangements for foreign clients for whom an accurate 'paper trail' was essential. The trainee's innocent suggestion that perhaps the first partner could simply ask his client to forward a copy of the signed document concerned was dismissed as being a sign of incompetence and weakness, and the trainee berated for not understanding this.

Just remember that this sort of behaviour is not your fault, make a note that this may not be the department you want to work in when you qualify and resolve not to treat trainees in this way when you are qualified.

MEMORY TEST

The purpose of this test is to demonstrate how quickly we forget oral instructions. You will need to recruit the assistance of three friends.

1. Read out the following list of 18 words to Friend One:
Memory
For
Water
The
House
For
Day
Tax
Tomb
Master
The
Exhilaration
For
New Zealand
Treat
For
Hockey
Soccer

After a minute ask your friend to write out the list of words.

2. Read out the list of words to Friend Two and ask Friend Two to write out the list of words after an hour.

3. Read out the list of words to Friend Three and ask Friend Three to write out the list of words after a day.
You will find that the number of words remembered will decrease with the elapse of time. The words that will be remembered will most likely be:
Words which are repeated
Words at the beginning and at the end of the list
The unusual word (New Zealand)

Of course if you had permitted your friends to write down the words as you dictated them, they would have been able to refer to the list to refresh their memories.

Chapter 9

IT'S A BUSINESS

SPEED READ SUMMARY

■ Firms need to bring in a substantial amount in fees to pay for office overheads as well as the salaries of their legal staff. Clients are billed at a set rate per hour according to the seniority of those carrying out the work.

■ You will be set a billing target of a set number of hours which the Finance department and the Management Committee have assessed should be sufficient to cover overheads and allow for profit.

■ You will be required to record the time that you have taken for any task so that the client can be billed appropriately. Your supervisors need to know how much time a task has really taken, so don't over-record or under-record your time. Avoid the temptation to inflate the amount of time that work has taken. This is fundamentally dishonest.

■ Bills go out to clients with a 'narrative' of the work performed. It's easier to write this if you keep notes as you go along.

■ See also Chapter 9 of *All you Need to Know about Commercial Awareness* by Chris Stoakes (See **Useful Books**, *p.229*).

BILLING

It is as well to realise as soon as possible that you are a commodity that your firm has purchased and that they will want to see a return on their investment. This investment is not just the salary they pay you, but also the time and money expended on recruiting and training you to do the job.

In addition your firm needs to see that you are billing enough to help pay for offices, support staff, training, insurance premiums, marketing and all the other expenses associated with running a law firm. These things don't come cheap and the commercial reality is that it is the money brought in by the 'fee-earners', including you, which pays for them. It therefore goes without saying that the more ways that you bring in fees for your firm, directly or indirectly, the more highly regarded you will be.

What do you need to do?

BILLING TARGETS

Fee-earners are usually billed out at a set rate per hour, which is decided on the basis of what a particular market will bear, so that you may find that the rate per hour of a City trainee is more than that of a High Street partner in a small town. The one thing that you can be sure of is that within a firm this set rate will increase with the seniority of the fee-earner.

Fee-earners are each given a 'billing target', which is a statement of the number of hours that they are expected to bill in any one year. On the whole this increases with seniority until partnership level is reached. Even if you are apparently not given a formal target because 'you are still a trainee', the firm will have an idea of the annual number of hours that it expects you to bill. Stated target hours in City firms vary between 1,300 and 1,750 and some include an additional amount for marketing and development.

WHERE YOUR TIME GOES

Multiplying your set rate per hour by the number of hours you are targeted to bill will give you an idea of the amount of money that the firm wants you to bring in. This will probably seem like a huge amount compared to your salary – but remember that whatever you receive as salary at the end of the month, you will probably be costing the firm at least another 20% more in National Insurance, pension contributions, health insurance and season ticket loans.

On top of paying your salary, the firm will also be paying for your office rent, your secretary's salary, your telephone, your computer and so on. In fact everything that you use, whether it be the vending machine or the 'free' gym membership, has to be paid for somewhere along the line. That's why you need to bill – a lot.

RECORDING TIME

On the whole clients are charged for the amount of time that their solicitors have spent on their work. There may well be additions for sophisticated expertise or urgency or subtractions for pro bono or as a loss-leader or because the person who is billing feels that it would be unfair to charge the time cost or knows that the client would not be able to pay all of it. However, the first thing that anyone looks at when deciding on the amount of a bill is the number of hours spent on the matter. Even if the client and the firm have agreed a fixed fee for the matter, the firm will still need to know the amount of time that has been spent as a guide to what they should be charging next time.

Initially you are going to take an extraordinary amount of time to do things, which with practice you will gradually learn to do much more quickly. This is particularly true with anything that involves 'forms', whether they are land transfers, company articles, stock transfer forms or wills. You need to familiarise yourself with the format and that takes time.

Dealing with forms

Although you will probably have looked at all these documents in your LPC most firms have their favourite forms, many have spent a huge amount of time and money tailoring them to their own requirements and these documents are getting longer, and longer, and longer as the law becomes more complex. Make sure that you read them very carefully before you start to fill them in. If you have only one copy of an original form, take a photocopy to practise on. And don't forget to copy or save, if it's an e-form, the completed original for the file before you send it off.

RECORD TIME ACCURATELY

Each time that you carry out some billable work, you will be required to record the amount of time that it has taken so that it can be charged against a client or matter number. Don't lie about the amount of time that you spend on something. Your supervisor may have a fair idea of how long it should take, and will not be amused if you put down two hours for something when it should have taken 15 minutes because you have been gossiping in the library. Equally if something has genuinely taken you a long time don't under-record, because you will then be in the position of having to explain why you are not putting in the hours the firm is paying you for. Or worse still there may well be an expectation that you can do the same amount of work in a very short period of time in the future.

Don't be tempted to put down less time than you have taken because you think that the client should not have to pay for your 'learning time'. It is up to the supervisor to write time off when it comes to billing the client.

When you have done something for the first time it's a good idea to make a note of the amount of time that it took. Having a rough idea of how much time a task takes can help you to manage your own time. If you don't know how long it is likely to take you to 'Pop down to the Court and get... ', how can you say whether you have the time to do it or not?

Get used to recording time, because when you are qualified you will find that in many firms your annual bonus, if any, may be linked to the hours you have billed. Don't put it off. As soon as you have finished a piece of work, assess how long it took you and record it. Even if it only took ten minutes, put it down, because unaccounted-for ten-minute chunks can add up to a great deal of lost profit for your firm and unappreciated time for you. There are many ways of recording time, whether on paper or through timing mechanisms linked to central recording. Make sure you understand exactly what is involved. It's just another good habit to learn.

You will find that in some firms there is a departmental Wall of Shame where those departmental members who have not met their targets by the end of the week or month have their names emblazoned for all to see. Ruthless perhaps, but it does indicate the importance of this aspect of your working day.

BILL NARRATIVES

When you are recording your time, make sure that you don't write tersely 'X Ltd – 30 minutes'. At some point someone, and it will probably be you, will have to prepare a bill for the client. Bills are not sent out saying simply, 'To legal services – £114,568'. People need to be reminded of what has been done for them, so the request for payment is accompanied by what is called a Bill Narrative. This is a summary of the work that your firm has carried out for the client on this particular matter. The detail that will be included will vary not only according to the amount of time spent on the matter, but also on the department (Private Client departments tend to send longer narratives), how frequently you do the same sort of transaction for a particular client and how sophisticated the client is.

The conveyancing work that you do for a first-time buyer may paradoxically require a longer narrative than the compliance work that you do for an offshore investment fund for whom you do the same sort of thing 20 times a year. But whoever the client is, and however long the narrative has to be, it will be much easier to write it if you have all the detail of what has been done to hand. Even if you are not the one to write the narrative, you will be able to give the relevant information and then get back to 'proper work' more quickly if your time recording has been done properly.

DISHONESTY

There is one practice, fortunately rare, that you may encounter and which you should not emulate. While you are recording your time honestly, you may feel that one of your supervisors is apparently inflating time to give an imaginative impression of the amount of work actually performed.

What do you do in this situation?

Most importantly, do not go around making wild accusations. There may be valid reasons for what you see as time inflation. Your supervisor may, for example, have an agreement with a client that over a number of similar transactions the bill for each will be roughly the same. The way that he ensures this is that he puts down roughly the same amount of time for each, even though he will be over-recording on some transactions and under-recording on more difficult ones. Or the matter may have dealt with a legally novel issue which although it may result in a superficially straightforward letter of advice may have involved your supervisor in a great deal of personal research and consultation, which has been lazily swept up in the simple statement 'background research – five hours'.

However, even if you are sure that time is being 'manufactured', don't be tempted to follow the example of the manufacturer. It takes only one important client querying a bill and a partner with a bit of time on his hands who decides to check its components and you could be found out. Senior lawyers have a reasonably shrewd idea of the amount of time that it takes you to do something, even taking account of your 'learning time'.

Chapter 10

PEOPLE WHO CAN HELP YOU

SPEED READ SUMMARY

■ Support staff tend to remain longer in a firm than lawyers. Consequently they are the 'folk memory' of the firm. Learning who they are and how they can help you will make you much more efficient.

■ Secretaries can help or hinder – often on a whim. Think carefully about what you can reasonably ask them to do and what you can do for yourself.

■ Professional Support Lawyers (or PSLs) are qualified lawyers who enjoy legal work but who, often for family reasons, do not want to do transactional work. They can be more experienced than the lawyers doing the transactions.

■ Non-legally qualified staff are essential for the smooth running of a legal office. Don't underestimate their ability to help you – or to damage your career.

■ Partners value stability in the office structure. Having to waste time on recruiting and keeping support staff happy is a great irritation.

■ The function of Human Resources is to manage the firm's prime resource – people. They are not substitute social workers.

SUPPORT POWER

When you enter the portals of your firm on your first day as a new trainee, you may indulge in a bit of fantasy that in ten years' time you will be a partner and that in 20 years it is you who will be running the show.

There are a whole lot of people who know better. Some of them will have been there since they left school and some will be there until they retire and most of them are not lawyers.

Support staff are essential to the smooth running of any firm. One of the easiest and most silly mistakes for new trainees to make is to assume that non-lawyers have no power. Some of them have known the most senior members of the firm since they themselves were trainees and may well be their trusted confidantes. They could also tell you about the foibles of these same senior people, but what is far more likely is that they will tell them about you. About your foibles, pranks and character defects (and illicit affairs if you disregard the advice in Chapter 6).

Support staff have a job to do in the firm as well as you and they deserve to be treated with courtesy. If your supervisor bawls you out, it is extremely unwise to take it out on your secretary or the post-room boy. Get used to the idea that they do not owe their jobs or their positions in the firm to you. Get used to knowing that they do not on the whole regard your work as urgent, even if your supervisor has just harangued you about how urgent it is. Get used to the idea that even if your supervisor has told them that your work is just as important as his, they will still put his first in the queue; after all you may be gone in a few months and he will still be there.

SECRETARIES

Even as a trainee you will normally have the luxury of secretarial assistance. However, secretaries usually work for more than one fee-earner of whom you will inevitably be the most junior. Having a good relationship with your secretary can make a substantial difference to your productivity and general wellbeing, but this will require some effort and sensitivity on your part.

Don't make a habit of trying to dump work on your secretary at 4.30 in the afternoon expecting it to be completed by 'close of play'. That is what your supervisor will be demanding. Not only will your work not get done, but you will resent the fact that it has not been done and your secretary will resent your asking. If matters are very urgent, then on an occasional basis your secretary may well be able to help you out or call in a favour from another secretary. But don't 'cry wolf'. Only say that your work is exceptionally urgent if it really is.

Remember to say thank you. You may have a glittering career ahead of you, but you will need the help of secretaries and support staff for many, many years. It's short-sighted (and inhuman) to treat your support staff as automatons. Don't be rude. It will get you nowhere. Staff talk to each other, so that not only will you get less co-operation from your own secretary, you will get none from anyone else's.

Remember little courtesies like sending postcards to secretaries when you are on holiday and Christmas cards and if possible a small gift.

Giving out work

Before you give any work to any secretary you have not worked with before, ask how your work should be presented.

Ask how they prefer you to dictate and how they would like documents to be marked up for correction.

Explain which partner each individual piece of work is intended for, as they will know how that partner likes the work presented.

If you have a major piece of work on which you need your secretary's help, give as much advance warning as possible. Agree a timetable:
- when you will submit it
- when you need the first draft back
- when it needs to go out

Do your best to stick to the timetable and you should have the making of an excellent working relationship.

Additional secretarial skills

Your secretary can tell you:
- What is going on in the office
- Which partner has a bark that is worse than his bite, and more importantly which partner's bite is worse than his bark
- What is the real power hierarchy in the office, which may not be the same as the Management Structure Chart
- Who are the best people to go to in the office for different tasks

Your secretary can also:

- Help you to fill in internal forms correctly so that your work is not returned several hours later from the print room or word processing because you have not ticked the appropriate box or entered a cost code.
- Ensure that one of the other secretaries will help you if your secretary is not available. But this will only happen if the other secretaries can be assured that you are appreciative and not difficult.
- Teach you about the office style and document short cuts. Don't for a moment think that this is beneath you. There will be situations where you will have to get a document out and there will be no one there to help you. Take for example the situation where your partner has promised a will to a client who is going abroad the next day. It is fairly straightforward, but a draft will have to be available for his perusal first thing in the morning. The secretaries in your office do not work beyond six pm. Do you think that it will be the partner who types up the first draft from the office precedent? No, it will be you. And there will be an implicit expectation, however unrealistic, that you will know how to do it and will be able to produce a perfect document.

Dictation

If it is the office's normal practice to use dictaphones so that secretaries type up documents from fee-earners' recordings, learn how to use one as quickly as possible. Writing your work out in longhand will take you longer, will take your secretary longer to type up and will often lead to massive irritation if your handwriting is difficult to read. Dictaphones are not difficult to get used to. If your supervisor hasn't explained how to use one, ask your secretary for guidance.

Ask for feedback from the typist on your first dictation tape. Once you are working in harmony with the secretaries you will find that your dictation comes back with far fewer mistakes because of misunderstandings. However, don't expect total perfection. Very few people are totally satisfied when they see the results of their dictation in cold print. What you should remember is that the whole process of getting your thoughts down on paper so that you can edit them proceeds far more efficiently if you can speak them clearly rather than writing them out laboriously by hand.

Don't forget that you can use your dictaphone to say thanks to the secretaries. One lawyer who used to use a large typing pool got to know the typists well enough to add on a relevant and cheerful comment to each tape. Her work always went to the front of the queue and seemed to come back with far fewer errors than anyone else's.

Helpful dictation

At the beginning of the recording identify:
- the matter number
- the client
- the author (in case the tape goes to the typing pool)
- the date
- the type of document

Matter Number 56/1234, client Tom Rice, dictated by Bill Bloggs, date 25 January 2008, this is a research note.

As you dictate you should indicate when the following are necessary:
- new paragraph
- new sentence
- quote and unquote
- italics
- bold
- headings

If you are dictating more than one piece of work on one tape, perhaps several short letters, make sure that you commence each item with the matter number, client, author, date and document details outlined above.

Tackle your own typing

There was a time when female trainees would not admit that they could type and would not learn to type in the first place in case they were treated as secretaries. It is now no longer in any trainee's interests, whether male or female, to be in this position. All trainees will have to do some of their own typing, especially now that so much work is done using email, but the skill now is in knowing what is sensible to do yourself and what should be left to a secretary or the Word Processing department. If you find yourself at a loose end one summer holiday, one of the best investments you can make in yourself is to learn how to touch type.

If you are familiar with office-style formatting you can do minor amendments yourself and this will often take up less time than strolling along to your secretary's room, explaining what you want, having it explained to you that it won't get done until later that day and then walking back to your own desk to wait for the amendments. On the other hand a long draft letter is often better dictated to your secretary in the first instance, simply because you should be able to talk faster than you can type. This is also the case if you are sending out a series of short letters. Setting up the page formatting and printing off the letters themselves and their accompanying envelopes take time, which you could better spend in researching or analysing the next legal problem on your list.

If you are typing a document yourself or amending one that your secretary has typed, make sure that you follow the agreed procedure for filing the most up-to-date electronic version. Your secretary will be frustrated and you will risk a mistake if you can't easily identify the most up-to-date copy on the system because the document is named incorrectly or several versions exist. Follow the naming etiquette and save it in the correct place.

If you lose a document because you accidentally hit the delete button or saved the wrong version, don't panic. The IT department often has wonderful ways of retrieving a document that you thought was gone forever. Often versions are saved intermittently on the hard drive as you type the document without you ever having to press Ctrl+S. However, if this happens at midnight and the document needs to be with the client by eight am then you may well have to resign yourself to a very late night retyping a complete document.

Precaution

Since what you type is usually intermittently saved on the hard drive without your realising it, it follows that you should not type anything that you would be embarrassed for your supervisor or the Managing Partner to see. Even if you think you have deleted it, it is probably still there somewhere on the firm's system.

Don't forget to check your secretary's work

You may think that it is tedious to look through letters and notes for typing errors, but it is better than having these errors come back to haunt you. Remember that:

- No client wants to find his or her name or address wrongly spelled on a letter.
- No other lawyer in your office wants to find his or her name wrongly spelled on a note.
- You should check any dates and numbers carefully. It is wiser in any

event to type out dates in full. A date of 11/10/2009 means 11 October to someone in the UK but 10 November to someone in America.

■ Bad grammar looks sloppy.
■ Your numbering should be consistent.
■ If you ask your secretary to make amendments for you, you should check that they have been made as you directed.

Always remember that the person who is ultimately responsible for the work that you send to your supervisor or the letter that goes out to a client is you. Your supervisor is supposed to check your work, but may be too rushed to do so properly, or may have come to rely on you to produce accurate and well-presented work. However, if on the one occasion that he does not check your work you have failed to check what your secretary has produced for you, your supervisor will not consider that the fault is his when the client phones in to tell him that the Completion Date should be 15 June and not 16 July, or that the pearl necklace was to be left to Daisy and not Diana.

And if such a mistake is made, the very last thing you should do is to blame the secretary. It looks cheap and pathetic; be big enough to accept responsibility yourself and make sure that you check more carefully in future.

Secretaries from Hell

Most secretaries are helpful if you are reasonable with them. If they cannot always comply with your requests it is usually because they have work to do for a partner or senior associate which takes precedence. However, there are some who seem to relish the brief power that they have over the trainee they are meant to be helping. One secretary took a perverse pleasure in handing notes from the supervising partner to his trainee just before she left at 5.30. Earlier in the day she would have typed the note requiring work to be done by ten am the next morning, but she 'forgot' to pass it on. The filing that she did for the trainee was usually out of order, if indeed it made it from the filing tray to the file. Needless to say what she did for the partner was immaculate, so there was no point in complaining.

Another secretary made it clear that no typing would be done by her for the trainee unless he first coloured in large complex plans for a shopping centre development first. This was a task that she had been given by the partner but which she heartily disliked. Again complaining to the very busy partner was fruitless because he had received what he asked for – letters from his trainee ready to be signed and a set of coloured-in plans. There may come a time when you are asked to contribute to the secretary's assessment when you can indicate mildly that she has been 'less than co-operative', but for the moment you may just have to console yourself that your time in that particular department is finite.

PROFESSIONAL SUPPORT LAWYERS

PSLs or Professional Support Lawyers are just that. They are qualified solicitors (or sometimes barristers), they are there to support the front-line troops and they are professional. It is a serious mistake to underestimate them.

A firm will employ a newly qualified solicitor to be part of a transactional team but would not choose a newly qualified solicitor to be a PSL. PSLs need to have some practical post-qualification experience in order not only to be able to lay their hands on, but to understand, relevant legislation and case law. A good PSL is part academic and part transactional lawyer, sometimes a tutor but with the organisational skills of a librarian. Although it varies from firm to firm their job descriptions might include:

■ Drafting precedents for transactional lawyers to use
■ Drafting marketing material for clients
■ Providing departmental newsletters to keep the transactional lawyers up-to-date on the latest case law and legislation
■ Setting up and maintaining a database of material relevant to the department's business ('Know-How') and making sure that that material is available and in good order when needed
■ Summarising the material that goes into the database
■ Acting as a sounding board for other lawyers in the department
■ Writing articles for professional journals
■ Preparing and giving seminars

You might well ask, if they can do so much, why then are they not involved with client work? There are as many reasons for this as there are PSLs.

Many PSLs are women who want to combine a satisfying occupation with looking after a young family. PSLs normally work more regular hours than transactional lawyers, which can enable them to get family and work more in balance. Some are partners coming up for retirement who enjoy the law but want to wind down gradually. Some have simply found that they have lost the taste for working with demanding clients.

Some want to combine working in the law with doing other things. As many firms are more willing to employ part-time PSLs than part-time transactional lawyers this can be an ideal solution for someone who wants to do voluntary work or acquire other skills and qualifications.

Your relationship with PSLs

In some firms there is a perceived loss of status attached to someone's opting to be a PSL. At any equivalent level of qualification it is certainly less well paid, and many PSLs can find it difficult not being part of a transactional team. Remember this when you are dealing with them, because they can give you a great deal of help – if they consider that it is part of their remit.

As you will see from the above description of what they might be asked to do, their days can be pretty full. Your breezing in with a peremptory request could be the last straw.

Like everyone else in a law firm they too need help from time to time. If you are at a loose end it might be possible, with your supervisor's agreement, to assist them and you will learn something in the process. Summarising case law or letters of advice for the know-how database may not seem very exciting to you when you are itching to get out there to take instructions from clients or to stride the corridors of the law courts, but you need to have something to impress the clients with and something to ask the court for. By helping your departmental PSL you could be increasing your stock of legal knowledge.

Remember that if you help your PSLs, they will also be more willing to help you.

What PSLs can do for you

In a firm with a sophisticated know-how system you should be able to obtain a great deal of departmental information from your desktop PC. However, the fact that you can call up all 370 letters of advice produced in the past two years by the firm's Private Client department on the topic of Capital Gains Tax on the sale of a family business will not necessarily be a great deal of help if you do not know what you need the information for.

A friendly PSL may help you to:
■ Isolate the pertinent points you should be searching for if you have not been given adequate instructions from your supervisor

- Help you to identify the questions to ask your supervisor to get better instructions so that you can ascertain the real point of the question
- Explain why there is a particular clause in a precedent
- Find the real name of the case that you have been asked to consider
- Find the up-to-date thinking on a topic
- Guide you on what to ask the firm's librarian if you need to consult the library holdings

PARALEGALS

This term covers broadly fee-earners who are not practising solicitors or barristers. They come from a variety of backgrounds. Some are legal executives, with formal legal qualifications from the Institute of Legal Executives (ILEX). Some have no formal legal qualifications, although others have qualified as solicitors or barristers but are not currently practising. Some LPC graduates accept a post as a paralegal hoping to be offered a training contract, and others are working as paralegals in one firm while waiting to take up a training contract which has already been arranged with another.

Don't assume that being a paralegal is second rate to being a trainee. Some paralegals will have as much experience and know-how in their particular field as the most senior partner in the firm. Stay on the right side of the paralegals as they can be a great source of help.

DEPARTMENTAL REPORTING

Secretaries, PSLs and paralegals will remain in the department after you have left. You will probably not return to that department and so will probably not have any long-term relationship with them. So, ask yourself, why is it in their interests to help you while you are in the department?

The answer is that it is of benefit if it helps the department to function well and smoothly. Like most people, they will also help you if it is in their power, if working with you is a pleasant experience. But if your requests are unreasonable or ill-conceived, if you think that they are some sort of emotional dumping-ground for your insecurities or petulance then you may get less than no assistance.

'Not very bright, is he?' or 'Not very well organised, that one,' are comments that might be thrown casually to your supervisor, but if said often enough will find their way on to your report. No senior lawyer wants dissension in his office, and he certainly does not want a disgruntled secretary or PSL. It can take long enough to find a secretary or PSL who works well within a department, but trainees come out of the law school machinery on a very regular basis and often there is an over-supply of them.

Document Exchange

Not all communication goes by email. A considerable amount still goes by snail mail or by the DX. DX stands for Document Exchange. This is a private mail network used by most law firms and chambers for business mail. Subscribers take their outgoing mail to and collect incoming mail from designated DX collection points. DX is generally regarded as more reliable and secure than the regular postal service. The downside is that although law firms and chambers subscribe, most other businesses do not. To secure next day delivery for your clients you will probably need to arrange Special Delivery or a courier. Ask your Post Room for advice.

POST ROOM

Firms have many different ways of dealing with post and not all firms have a dedicated Post Room. In smaller firms it will be the secretaries or the trainees who go to the Post Office to mail parcels and items which have to go by Recorded Delivery. Although you clearly don't want to take more than your fair share of this sort of work, more than is undertaken by other trainees or secretaries, it is better to accept with a good grace that like Wells Fargo the mail has to get through. Otherwise there was no point in doing the work in the first place.

Remember that sole practitioners have to do all this sort of work themselves. If you are working in a small firm and want to be kept on, remember that your complaining will have been noted by everybody, and it will not operate in your favour. So, take your turn but also make sure that that when it is the posting hour at least some of the time you are doing 'absolutely won't wait until tomorrow' work.

In a small firm have a close look at how the post is managed. Is there any way that its collection and dissemination could run more smoothly? Would it be possible for you to come in a bit earlier in the morning and then leave earlier so that you could take the post to the Post Office or the DX on the way home?

Large firms on the other hand can afford to operate a dedicated internal mail service, which delivers and collects items of post and also carries messages and documents between fee-earners in the firm. This will variously be delivered to your desk, to your secretary, or to a dedicated pigeon hole in a central collection point on your floor. It is important that you know where this is and roughly at what time the post is delivered. If your post is delivered to your secretary rather than to you, you could find yourself waiting for an important piece of mail, perhaps answers to enquiries you have made of a vendor's solicitors, if she is off because of illness or a traffic jam or she is too busy to walk round to your office with it. Go and check. It's your responsibility, not hers.

It can be tricky if you are waiting for a crucial piece of information but all incoming mail has to be seen by the partner first and the partner has not come in yet or is in a meeting. If you are on good terms with the partner's secretary, she may be willing at least to find out if the letter has come in, and even better to let you see it. But do this only if the matter is really important, and explain to the secretary why you are making this request.

Don't:

- Shout at the Post Room boys (they are usually male) if the mail is a few minutes late, or the letter that you want has not yet arrived from the outside world. It may mysteriously happen more often.
- Wander into the Post Room uninvited without knocking first. Post Room staff may have been working there for many years. They will never earn a lot of money, but the Post Room is their space and they do not usually welcome an unannounced intrusion into their private territory.
- Think that they will put themselves out for you just because you are a trainee and will one day be a solicitor. They know that you may not even have a job at the end of your training contract, while they will still be there. You should always be polite.
- Send your personal mail to be franked (and paid for) via the firm's Post Room. In many firms this is a sackable offence, and even if you don't get caught, your supervisor probably knows you've been doing it. Always pay for your personal mail. Post Room will probably weigh and send your personal mail as long as you pay for it out of your own pocket, which can save you hours of queuing at your local Post Office. But remember that they are not obliged to do this, and if they don't want to, they won't.

Do:

- Find out what they can do for you. They will know what is the best and cheapest way for an item to be dealt with. Before you airily spend the firm's money on a courier, they will be able to tell you whether Post Office Special Delivery would do the job just as well.
- Consult the Head of the Post Room politely, who may then be willing to go that extra mile for you (literally) when you have something that needs to go out urgently.
- Put yourself in their shoes. Your urgent item is just another item in sackfuls of mail that they deal with in any one day. Why should they disrupt the even tenor of their day just for you? An urgent item not being sent out that evening may be disastrous for you, but it will not have much of an effect on their future employment unless you can show that they have been deliberately obstructive.
- Take a genuine interest in the person who is delivering your mail. He has a life outside the office and you may just find that you have interests in common such as music or sport. If he can identify you in a positive way, rather than 'that difficult trainee in X's department' you will both have a much easier life.

PRINT ROOM

Many of the same injunctions apply to the Print Room. However, here you are dealing with people who have to work under significant pressure, probably in an uncomfortable space, and who have had a substantial amount of training in order to do their job. As well as photocopying masses of documents for meetings and to send out to clients, they may also have the capability to produce professional brochures for marketing or other purposes.

They are usually housed in the basement of the firm's offices, surrounded by a fair amount of noise and stacks of paper and equipment. Indeed the equipment that they operate often requires manuals the size of a textbook which they have to find their way through. It is not all about pressing a button, but about considering complex settings before that button is pushed.

In some smaller offices the Print Room staff may be willing to show you how to do simple tasks so that you can do them yourself. Although you do not want to be doing this all the time, it can be useful if you are up against a deadline or it is after hours. Above all, always give Print Room staff as much notice as possible of a job that you want them to do.

Don't:

■ Badger Print Room staff to get things done for you. They have a priority system which can be just as ferocious as yours. If you need something to be done urgently (and remember that not everything is really urgent) then phone up and ask whether you can take something down to them.

■ Toss something into the out tray at six or seven pm with a note of instruction that you need ten copies for 9.30 the next day, just because you know that Print Room carries on overnight. It may not get picked up because the Post Room has shut down for the night, and even if it does get delivered, it will probably be added to the pile of other non-urgent things to be looked at the next day. Phone up first to check that they can do the work for you, and then be prepared to deliver it yourself; and don't forget to say thank you.

Do:

■ Explain why you need something completed by a particular date and time. Remember that in order to look after the work of the whole firm they need to work out their own schedules.

■ Say which partner you are working for if you have been given a deadline by a partner. They will know even better than you what will be the effect of that work not being done on time. Some partners will have a spectrum of acceptable time, but others will have a Vesuvius eruption if something is half an hour late. The Print Room wants to be efficient just as much as you do.

■ Give them as much warning as possible if you know that you have a large printing and copying job for a particular date. Don't leave it until the last minute to let them know. If Print Room know that there will be a large job or, worse still, several large jobs to be done over a day or couple of days they can ensure that all preparation work is done, extra staff drafted in, all other work done up-to-date, and legal staff warned that routine photocopying that could be done by trainees or secretaries may not be able to be done over that period.

WP

WP stands for Word Processing. Most large firms will have dedicated members of staff who deal with typing up and amending large documents, especially after hours, or else they outsource this work to firms who specialise in providing WP services. WP also act as a back-up for secretaries who do a great deal more for their fee-earners than typing and dealing with documents.

It is a very good idea to find out the way that they like to operate. About six weeks into her training contract one mature trainee sent down a document to WP which had been amended in the way that she was accustomed to in her previous employment – she had attached various handwritten pieces of paper in what is known as a 'cut and paste job'. She was summoned by the head of WP, where in front of an amused assembly her work was fluttered in her face and she was asked 'Are you a trainee or a secretary?' She never did find out the precise significance of this question, but she had just sufficient presence of mind to ask meekly how WP preferred work to be sent down. Peace was made and she found afterwards that her work was consistently shunted to the front of the line.

RECEPTION

Receptionists are the first people that anyone sees when they enter your firm's offices. In a very small office the receptionist may well have other functions, such as being secretary to one of the fee-earners or office manager or telephonist. Larger firms may have a whole battery of them.

Receptionists give the first impression of the firm and are recognised as doing so. In large firms they wear a distinctive uniform and will probably be the only members of the firm's staff to do so. You may think that they are simply 'meeters and greeters' whose function is only to smile at everyone, but that would be a big mistake.

Receptionists are often responsible for the allocation of rooms for meetings. Remember that as a trainee you will have very little standing when it comes to commanding such rooms, and will probably have very little need to ask for them. However, you may have to ask on behalf of your supervisor, and if you have been polite to the receptionists when you arrive in the morning, and notice that they have been off on holiday, you may find that it becomes surprisingly easy to access the room allocations.

Receptionists are responsible for telling you that your client has arrived and is waiting in reception. They can helpfully give you information about how the client looks that morning, or if you have not met the client before, what the client actually looks like, information that can assist in your giving the right impression when you greet the client. It's useful to know things like 'Mr X doesn't like to be met by anyone other than Mr Z, the Head of Department, so he is going to frown at you and grumble, but don't take it personally,' or 'She's come with a baby in tow.'

Making life difficult

Remember that an undervalued receptionist can make life difficult in many little ways. They can:

- 'Forget' to tell you that the client has been in reception for 15 minutes.
- Phone your supervisor to say that the client is in reception when you have given instructions that you are to be called first. If a receptionist smiles sweetly and says that 'Your phone was engaged' or that 'You didn't answer your phone', you can hardly stand in reception and have a 'no, it wasn't, yes it was', slanging match. It's far better to ensure that no receptionist has a reason to behave like this with you.
- Neglect to inform you that the urgent package that you have been waiting for has just been couriered in. A variation on this is to put the package into internal mail where it may take another three hours before it surfaces on your desk.

And making life easy

However, a receptionist who feels that you are on the same side can:

- Find meeting rooms when none seem to be available.
- Make an effort to find you when the client arrives. If your phone is engaged she will phone your secretary and if you are both engaged will send you an email and additionally leave a message with someone else's secretary in the department.
- Be especially helpful with your clients, and talk you up in little ways.

You may well not be aware of what is going on here. After all these are little things that are happening in a part of the building which may well be several floors away. But just because you do not know about them, do not think that they do not happen.

AND INTO THE FUTURE

Don't imagine that you can be rude to any of the support staff when you are a trainee and that somehow when you are qualified they will kow-tow to you and fulfil your every unreasonable whim. It simply does not work like that. Support staff whom you have alienated or upset will have ways of getting their own back at you for years to come of which you will be simply unaware, but which added up over the years may come to a hefty sum of inconvenience for you.

HUMAN RESOURCES

This department used to be called Personnel, but is now called Human

Resources or simply HR. You will not usually find HR professionals in smaller firms, where one of the partners will take responsibility for those who are on the legal advice-giving team and the office manager will look after everyone else.

Their title may seem a bit of modern inflation speak for something much simpler, like refuse operative for dustman, but it does in fact indicate something that you should bear in mind in your dealings with them. The employees of the firm are a 'resource' available to the owners of the firm.

HR are there to assist the partners of the firm to maximise the profits of the firm by assisting management to deal with tricky issues involving its employees, by advising on employment law, by gathering statistics relevant to those employees (Why is our turnover of solicitors at three years PQE higher than that of other firms of comparable size? Why is sickness absence higher in litigation than in other departments?), by examining the applications of potential trainees and recently qualified solicitors, by conducting the first interviews with them, by liaising with recruitment consultants, by attending graduate recruitment fairs and most of all by ascertaining what it is that the partners are looking for in their staff.

Comfort providers?

HR are not there to ensure that you are happy or to be a shoulder for you to cry on, except in so far as your happiness impacts on the profitability of the firm.

Remember this before you start taking complaints to them. In very few cases will a conversation with HR be guaranteed to be completely private and confidential.

Also remember that they have procedures to go through. If you ask for informal advice on how to deal with a partner whom you feel is coming too close to you when reviewing your work, you may find that this could escalate into a formal complaint against him. It could also result in the partner concerned making a formal complaint about your work as part of a defence strategy.

Before you go to HR about anything other than advice about formalities, ask yourself whether there is anywhere else that you could get the information/help/good counsel that you need. You may well find that other trainees have felt uncomfortable in the presence of the partner you are concerned about. They may have advice on how to deal with the situation.

But...

At the same time, remember that in a large firm with many trainees and young solicitors, certain parts of HR could be vital to your professional progress in the firm. They can to a certain extent control your next seat as a trainee or your possible posting to an overseas office. Like everyone else they will have their favourites. At firm sports and quiz-night events you will probably have opportunities to socialise with the junior members of the HR team, and they may well be the same age as you. It does not take much effort to be polite and chatty, to find some common ground for conversation, and it could leave them with a useful favourable impression next time staff movements are discussed.

CLERKS IN CHAMBERS

Although clerks in barristers' chambers are not part of your village, they can smooth your way in other little villages. Remember that they are not administrative assistants; they take a very active part in the running of the chambers system and can earn more than many qualified solicitors, and usually more than many of the barristers that they work for. Their job is to deal with the workload and the finances of all barristers in their chambers from pupils to QCs.

As a trainee you will probably have little contact with chambers clerks, except that you might be asked to phone them to see when Mr X's opinion is likely to be ready, or whether Miss Y might be available for a telephone 'con' (remember that you have a consultation with a QC, but a conference with any other barrister). Resist any temptation to be stroppy with a chambers clerk. They are the gatekeepers to counsel, and you need access.

Clerks negotiate the 'brief fees' of their barristers and they are very experienced at this. It is not likely to be a trainee's job to get involved in any discussion about how much your firm should be paying a particular barrister for a particular piece of advice, drafting or court appearance, although you can start to form a picture of how much particular barristers charge and for doing what by noting the size of their fees when your clients are invoiced. Barristers bill their instructing solicitors and the solicitors pass on the bills to the client as part of their own bill. Find out if your firm has a preferred set of chambers or list of barristers and if there

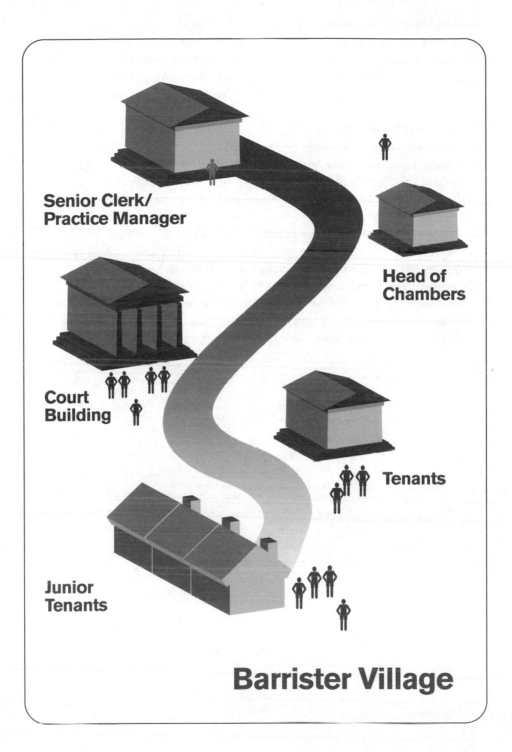

Senior Clerk/
Practice Manager

Head of
Chambers

Court
Building

Tenants

Junior
Tenants

Barrister Village

is a standard fee or charging agreement for that barrister or set of chambers. You might not be the one who chooses the barrister or sets the fee but your client may well ask you about the barrister or the fee. You ought to know, although this is probably not a topic for detailed discussion with the client without the permission of your supervisor.

You can negotiate – politely – to have one particular barrister rather than another. But this will depend very much on the type of work that your firm is engaged in. If you are working in the tax department of a large City firm, then it is likely that there will already be a relationship between your partners and particular barristers. When getting 'counsel's opinion' your firm will effectively be paying for a massive stamp of approval for a scheme or plan that they have in mind, or simply because the consequences of getting something wrong for one of their clients is immense. In a smaller criminal practice, your firm will be much more dependent on which barrister happens to be available, and the relationship that your firm has built up over the years with the chambers clerk is crucial here. If your firm is a good source of fees and pays promptly, then you are more likely to get the 'best available'.

Chapter 11

RAINMAKING AND NETWORKING

SPEED READ SUMMARY

- Networking is all about making new contacts. Rainmaking is an advanced form of networking that no one expects you to be able to do until you are much more senior.

- To be successful at both you need to be genuinely interested in people and also an interesting person to be with. You also need to take the time to prepare for networking events, to liaise with your colleagues beforehand and to pace yourself.

- It is equally important to follow up after an event by sending emails and making arrangements for future meetings if appropriate.

RAINMAKING

A 'rainmaker' is someone whose main function in a law firm is to get new business for that firm. Rainmakers often seem to have an apparently mystic power to increase their firms' profitability and are often gifted with charismatic personalities, but if you look more closely you will find that they achieve their status and high returns for their firms by understanding the needs of potential clients and by being interested in them.

Garlanded with high salaries, the lives of rainmakers may seem glamorous, but successful rainmaking is also hard work. Partners who are primarily engaged in rainmaking may look as though they have a cushy job, spending less time on the daily legal grind than other lawyers, but the reality is that they probably sacrifice a lot of time with their families, travel a lot more than they would like, have too many late nights and too much champagne and canapés thrust upon them (yes, that really is possible).

NETWORKING

Networking and rainmaking are very closely allied and you should consider rainmaking as an advanced form of networking.

Getting it done

Be proactive. When you start chatting to people, ask them about themselves:

- what do they do
- how did they get into that line of work
- do they enjoy it
- how do they see their business developing

Listen (this requires you to concentrate fully) and see where the conversation flows. Sometimes you will be amazed to find how many things you have in common, such as where you studied or a mutual interest in Modigliani or scuba-diving. As you become more confident, you will learn how to explore various different conversational avenues before you find something that you are both comfortable with.

When it is your turn to describe what you do, make sure that you give an interesting, but not a negative, response. Moaning about how much work your firm expects you to do, or that your landlord has just given you notice to quit, is a fast way to clear the space around you. The most successful networkers on the other hand light up a room because they are relaxed and genuinely happy to be meeting and greeting people.

As a trainee you are unlikely to be rainmaking, although no firm will object if you bring in a new fee-paying client, but there is an expectation that you will be engaging with others outside the firm to raise the firm's profile and to make new contacts. This is what networking is all about. If you are fortunate enough to be invited to a corporate hospitality day at Wimbledon or to a champagne reception at the Institute of Directors, do not think it is merely an opportunity for a jolly – this is networking with the emphasis on the middle syllable – **work**.

PREPARATION

What exactly does networking involve? Networking is about building up contacts who can be useful to you and to your firm and to whom you and your firm can be useful. Good relationships with accountants, surveyors or in-house counsel in large organisations can often be mutually beneficial.

To network effectively you need to spend time preparing for events to which you have been invited. Know what the event is about and who is likely to be there. Do a little background reading, for which a quick Google search will usually suffice, to find out something about likely attendees at an event hosted by your firm. If you are attending an event hosted by someone else, you should also try to find out as much as you can about the hosts. This will ensure that when you get there, you will already have formed some idea of things that you might have in common with the attendees and of ways in which your firm might assist or collaborate with them.

Dress appropriately for the event. The choice for men is usually a smart suit, but for women dressing appropriately for an evening event, a race meeting or an afternoon garden party can be more complicated. If you are not sure, check the dress code with a senior associate in your firm. Wearing the right thing is important if you want to feel confident and comfortable. At a sporting event where you are likely to participate, such as a golf day or a cricket match, you will need both the correct sporting gear and something smarter to change into afterwards.

Make sure you have business cards ready in your wallet or handbag. Although some people prefer to enter contact details straight onto their Blackberry or PDA, just as many people still like to exchange traditional business cards. It takes less time and is less likely to interrupt the flow of conversation.

BE RELAXED

Networking should look effortless. Do not be pushy. You are not there to

force yourself or your firm on anyone through a hard-sell sales pitch –
what most people like is to meet others who are genuinely interested in
them and who are interesting in themselves.

Note the word **genuinely**. If you are not actually interested in people,
then networking will be very hard work. Most people can tell instinctively if
someone else's interest is feigned. If they need your business, then they
will carry on the conversation, but otherwise they will simply turn away.

CIRCULATING

Moving around the room so that you get to speak to as many people as
possible is an art in itself. There is no hard and fast rule about how much
time you should spend with any one person; learn to sense when a
natural break in a conversation occurs. The person you are talking to
probably doesn't want to be monopolised by you any more than you want
to monopolise them. However, try not to walk away and leave someone on
their own – that is rude. Instead make an introduction to someone else
and then politely say, 'Would you excuse me. I am just going to go over to
say hello to X.'

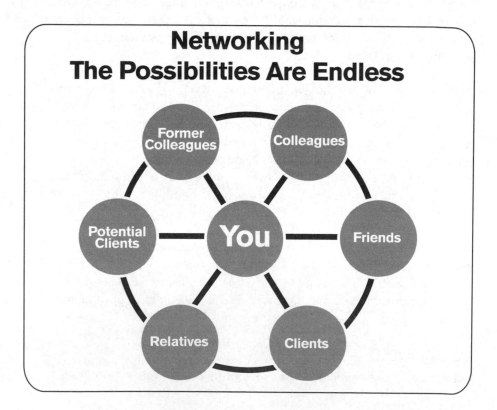

Networking rules

■ Be prepared
■ Be genuine, be genuinely interested and be interesting
■ Don't appear desperate or pushy
■ Be yourself and be positive
■ If you have made a congenial contact, remember to follow up afterwards

It is perfectly understood that you will have to break into other people's conversations, but it is wise not to break into groups of only two people. If you introduce yourself to a conversational duet, you may get an annoyed response because they were engaged in a serious conversation, or you may suddenly find that one of them immediately detaches herself, leaving you with a crashing bore.

Networking in pairs is often easier, because it is more relaxing to walk into a room with someone. It also doubles your chances of meeting new people, because your colleague can introduce you to a new contact and then continue to circulate. You can also keep an eye on each other to see if rescue is required through the simple expedient of asking politely, 'May I just steal Brenda for a moment as there is someone I would like her to meet.'

AFTER THE EVENT

Always ask people who are likely to be useful contacts for their business cards and record their details when you return to the office. If you have a genuine reason to contact someone you have met, if perhaps you were asked for more information about your firm or you agreed to fix a date to play squash, then follow up within a day or two. You should indicate where and when you met in your contact email or letter ('It was good to meet you at such and such last Tuesday') and follow up with a short description of what was agreed and suggestions for a further meeting.

Even if you have made no arrangements or there is no reason for you to contact anyone, find a means of storing all the business cards you have acquired with some useful notes, as you never know when this information might come in handy.

Inevitably some events will turn up more useful new contacts than others. Accept this; that is just the way it is. Sometimes an event that gave you high hopes will leave you disappointed and the one that you think will be boring will leave you pleasantly surprised. You just never know, so approach all events with an open mind. It is a numbers game; the more people you meet, the more chance you have of building a good set of contacts. Not everyone you meet at a networking event is going to turn into a potential client so don't try to force that – as long as people walk away with a favourable impression of you and your firm that is enough.

As your confidence, contacts and reputation as a lawyer increase, networking will turn into rainmaking. Develop your networking skills now!

Chapter 12

A SPORTING CHANCE

SPEED READ SUMMARY

- The organisation and promotion of sport can tell you a great deal about a firm and how it views itself, its clients and its staff. The sociology of corporate Golf Days is fascinating, and is probably why many female solicitors get so hung up on their apparent exclusivity.

- Think about the real marketing purpose of client sporting events and how they enhance client relationships. When you are invited as part of the support function at other client entertainments stay sober and discreet.

- Participating in sports outings organised by the firm for its staff is cheap entertainment and can help you to get to know other people in the office.

- Keeping in touch with friends who work in other offices and non-legal environments can be an important reality check and stop you being sucked into a narrow life.

SPORTING SOCIOLOGY

Sport, participating in it and discussing it, can play just as much a part of the social lubrication of office life as it did at school, university or college. In many ways it can be even more important as it facilitates networking and enables law firm villagers to get to know each other more easily. How a firm organises its 'sporting events', whether internally or as part of a marketing strategy, can tell you a lot about that firm.

GOLF

Playing golf is part of networking, but networking is more than playing golf.

This may seem obvious but it is amazing how hung up people, especially women, get about golf in law firms. Many female lawyers see golf courses as the ultimate boys club where deals are done, and use this example endlessly when discussion turns to the exclusion of women from marketing opportunities.

It only takes a moment's reflection to realise how very strange this really is. Golf must surely be the most egalitarian sport where women are concerned. Because of the handicapping system women and men can

Choosing players

Looked at objectively you would surmise that if a firm is truly interested in the wellbeing of its clients on the course, then it will make sure that at least some of its best players are included, even if they are trainees. But some firms take a very different view and consider that attendance at one of their Golf Days is some sort of prize for clients as well as its solicitors rather than thinking of them as opportunities for marketing and cementing client relationships. Some firms have been known:

■ Never to include trainees, even if they have good handicaps and have been working closely with some of the guests

■ To be so completely sold on their only male golfers policy, that they do not take along someone who has a University Blue in Golf because that person happens to be a woman

■ Not to invite any client more than once. They would rather cancel their Golf Day than disturb this policy

Most firms are not so short-sighted, so if you really do play golf, make it known. If you have a decent handicap certainly make that known. If someone in your family is a famous golfer, make that known as well — basking in reflected sporting glory is certainly allowed. You could be useful to the firm, if only because they introduce you as 'the brother of Y who played in the Ryder Cup team' or 'the cousin of X who was opening bat in the last Ashes tour.'

play it on fairly equal terms. Indeed it is possible to argue that it is the only sport that men and women, and young and old, the highly skilled and the relatively inept can play together on an equal footing. So what's the problem about golf?

Perhaps the problem is not with golf itself but with the difference between male and female attitudes to exposing weaknesses. If male lawyers are invited to a Golf Day by a client they are often so pleased to have an opportunity to get out of the office for the day that they forget that they do not really know how to play the game, and use the invitation to an expensive and prestigious golf club as an opportunity to practise their hacking techniques for several hours. (If you are sitting with such a partner, be careful what you say to him the morning after such an outing; it may have been an exhausting day of the utmost humiliation.)

Women on the other hand tend to turn down such an invitation if they know that their golf skills are inadequate or non-existent.

The reality is that some men invited on a Golf Day actually want to have at least one woman around. They see it as a guarantee that the behaviour at dinner afterwards will be civilised.

FIRM FORENSICS

You can tell a lot about a firm simply by looking at which of its staff are invited on Golf Days. Think for a minute about the purpose of such outings. People do not usually conclude business during a golf game, whatever you see in the cinema, but they do get to know each other better and the experience should leave clients with a set of pleasant memories.

Clients should feel that the purpose of a Golf Day to which they have been invited has been to give them a good time and that the people they have been playing with have been attentive, praising their good shots and looking for their errant balls. This is more likely to happen if the client is being looked after by a junior lawyer who happens to be a reasonable golfer than a senior lawyer who is an absolute beginner and is becoming increasingly frustrated by his own golfing shortcomings.

If you are invited to participate, remember that the whole object of the exercise is not to score the round of your life, but to entertain the client. The purpose of your being there is not to win the individual trophy of the day, but to help the client to win a team trophy with you. Indeed at any event where you are entertaining clients, the main focus of your attention must be the client.

OTHER SPORTS

Remember that firms also use other sports to build client relationships. Most firms regularly organise outings to sporting events for their clients and contacts, such as visits to football and rugby matches or to Henley or the University Boat Race.

Whatever the sport the underlying purpose is the same. It is about bonding, about showing the firm in a good light and building up good relationships with clients. At their worst, outings to rugby and football events may be fairly barbaric, because there is no requirement to stay sober enough actually to do anything, and the drinking may begin on the coach that takes the party to the event and continue well after it has ended.

As a trainee or junior lawyer you could be invited to such an outing in order to 'help' by looking after the clients, organising the programmes or handing round the beers and other refreshments. There is one cardinal rule in this situation: stay sober! Learn to 'nurse' your drink, which is also a good trick to learn for other marketing occasions. It will not create a good impression in anyone's mind if you are the rowdiest, or the sickest, or the most obnoxious person there. Even though partners may laugh at your behaviour in a paternalistic fashion afterwards, you will be unlikely to be invited again for a very long time. And they may have reservations about taking you to other non-sporting events.

TEAM SPORTS

Many firms encourage their younger staff to organise team games such as rugby, football, softball or rounders against teams from other firms or teams of assorted clients. If the firm is big enough it may organise leagues or tournaments as part of an internal bonding exercise.

As this is an opportunity for younger members of the firm to learn about each other and about other members of the firm, the firm is usually willing to pay for reasonable refreshments afterwards. If your firm does not already have this in place, you might suggest it – but only if you are prepared to take on the burden of arranging it.

The temptation is to use these outings as a cheap way to have an evening getting plastered, but this is not necessarily wise, especially if there are potential clients present or you have a busy day ahead of you. The paid refreshments situation illustrates one of the big problems with being a trainee. Most of the time you are treated as a thinking human being, albeit one who is a little inexperienced, but every now and then you are given an opportunity to have a college bad-behaviour day. Only take this opportunity if you are willing to be the butt of office jokes for some time to come, and 'for some time to come' can mean years in some cases.

However, such occasions are wonderful sources of gossip and often give you an opportunity to get to know People Who Can Help You in a more friendly way. Don't underestimate the importance of getting to know partners outside the office, whether on the golf course, at a rugby match or at an art show. Given the choice of two equally capable trainees to take to a client meeting or to take notes on an overseas visit, a partner is more likely to take the trainee with whom he can have an easy conversation about common interests during the inevitable 'down-times'.

ALL YOUR LEISURE?

The great temptation in a large firm village is not to look beyond the village. It is easy to spend your whole day there, cocooned in the comfort of free coffee, subsidised meals, dry cleaning services and organised recreation. But there is a wider world out there, and it is important not to lose touch with your friends outside the office, whether they are trainees in other firms or are engaged in other occupations entirely.

It takes time and effort to do this in a way that was not necessary at university, but it is vitally important to your sanity. You can share your experiences with friends in other offices (although clearly not details about your clients) and obtain a valuable perspective on what is 'normal' in a legal office. It's comforting to know for example after you have just spent two days preparing 'bundles' for a forthcoming court case that your friend in another firm has just spent three doing exactly the same thing.

And if when you have qualified you are thinking of moving to another firm it's useful to have some insider information on the character of the partners in the other firms who might be interviewing you. That is something that no recruitment consultant is likely to tell you even if they are in a position to know, because it is the other firm that will be paying their fees not you.

Do try to keep in touch with friends in other occupations who can give you another perspective on the world of work. If you are thinking that a legal career is not for you, it's useful to have a reality check against the experiences of non-legal friends. Is it really the law that is the problem, is it your firm, or is it just coming smack up against the restrictions of working in one place with the same people for 46 weeks of the year? Don't underestimate the culture shock that moving from the more fluid environment of student life to the more regimented one of the legal office can produce. Keeping in touch with friends who are not lawyers can help you to overcome this.

Chapter 13

ORGANISATION AND COMMUNICATION

SPEED READ SUMMARY

■ In order to succeed in a legal office you need to be organised and to plan ahead, using your diary to prioritise and to inform other people of what you are doing.

■ Telephones have a business purpose. Think carefully about how and whether to use them to speak to clients or friends.

■ Emails can ensure fast communication, but also confused communication. Recognise the difference between in-office and out-of-office email substance and protocol.

THE IMPORTANCE OF DIARIES

Successful lawyers are organised lawyers; they either organise themselves or rely on other people to get them organised. If you are a trainee, the onus will fall on you, both to organise yourself and to organise the partners and other lawyers that you work with.

If you have up to now relied on a paper diary, losing it will have had adverse consequences only for you. However, if it constitutes the only record of your work appointments and the deadlines that you must meet, other people could be very seriously affected by its loss.

This is why most offices now use electronic diaries. This in itself is insufficient if you do not make sure that your diary is backed up. Remember to sync your handheld PDA to your PC on a daily basis.

Electronic diaries are often set up so that others in the office such as your secretary and your supervisor have 'read access' to your calendar. They may also have the ability to enter dates in your diary, i.e. 'write access'. Difficult as you may find it to get used to the e-diary, because you have been using a paper diary for the last ten or 15 years, you will simply have to get used to it if that is the way the office works.

The added benefit of an e-diary is that it can be synced to a wireless handheld PC/PDA and you can see immediately the up-to-date position of your diary even when you are away from your office. The downside is of course that others may see the current state of your social life if you also use the e-diary to record it.

CALENDAR MANAGEMENT

To be really useful your diary should contain not only meeting dates and deadlines but also advance reminders of what you need to do to meet them. If you put a trial date in your diary, you should think backwards from that date and enter every single thing that needs to be done in advance to make sure you are prepared:

- contact witnesses to remind them where to attend and when
- update counsel's brief
- file the skeleton argument
- prepare and agree the bundle
- file the bundle
- confirm the time estimate and so on...

Whenever you enter an event in your diary, stop to consider all the preceding events that need to happen to ensure that the main event runs smoothly and enter those in your diary as well. Even if this is something as apparently simple as booking a table for a pre-Christmas lunch for your partners and counsel, remind yourself to check the day before both with the restaurant and with counsel's clerk that everything is arranged and agreed.

PHONE CALLS

Just as you can hear what your supervisor is saying on the telephone and may learn something of legal or of purely scurrilous interest by listening, remember that you too can be heard. Don't assume that just because your supervisor looks engrossed in a Share Sale Agreement he is not being attentive to your conversation.

If you are talking to a client your supervisor should be keeping at least half an ear on your conversation, to make sure that you are not giving negligent or inaccurate advice or indeed any advice at all in some cases. After all, your effectiveness in dealing with clients on the telephone will form part of your appraisal. Your supervisor will also note what you are saying to your friends and whether you are spending too much time on the telephone to them. And don't think that your supervisor is too busy to mull over what you have said about your weekend and then repeat it to the next person you are going to work for. Gossip is the lifeblood of village culture and law offices are no exception.

RECEIVING PHONE CALLS

Law firms have various different methods of dealing with phone calls. Some have DDI numbers (the calls are put straight through to you as though you had a private phone) and others insist that the call goes through to switchboard first. This has the advantage that the caller can be asked to give his name and he is then 'announced' by switchboard which gives you the opportunity to decide whether you will take the call, and also a little breathing space in which to raid your memory banks for information about the caller.

If your calls are received on a DDI number, you will have to develop a professional sounding introduction. 'Hi' will not do, as the caller may have phoned a wrong number, or might be the Chairman of Sony (very unlikely). Simply giving your name followed by a short pause will suffice. There is no need to adopt the 'How can I help you?' pose and also no need to recite your telephone number or to recite the name of the firm.

With DDI numbers you will not have the voicemail opt-out and will on some occasions have to 'cut the caller off at the pass' before they have said too much if you are engaged in a discussion with a partner who has come to your office to speak to you. Remember as you do this, that the partner will be assessing how politely you deal with the caller. 'I'm afraid that I'm just rushing out to a short meeting. Where are you phoning from so that I can get back to you?' will do.

DEFERRING COMMUNICATION

If you are busy, rushing to a deadline or discussing a matter with your supervisor, it is acceptable to ask the switchboard to put the caller through to your voicemail or to your secretary, but only if:

- You are sure that the caller will not be offended
- You are sure that the matter is not likely to be urgent
- You know that you can get back to the caller quickly

LISTENING AND WRITING

When you take a phone call keep paper and pen in front of you. It's always more professional to be able to take down notes without having to ask the caller to wait until you have located a writing implement. Then don't lose the paper! File it where you can find it, and if possible dictate a short note of what was said which can be placed on file and will have the benefit of being legible. Don't assume that other people can read your scribbled notes, or even that you will be able to do so yourself after some time has passed.

Repeat back telephone numbers and also the spelling of names and addresses if you are not absolutely sure of them, and make sure that you take down the caller's requirements accurately. You may hear the words 'new house purchase' but what the client actually wants is for a new will to be drafted leaving the house he has just bought to his daughter. It's very easy for misunderstandings to arise in telephone conversations, so be careful. If you take down a telephone number incorrectly from someone who is looking for a firm to help with debt collection, what could have been a potentially lucrative client relationship could be lost as no one will be able to make subsequent contact.

As a general rule don't type whilst speaking on the phone to the client as the constant tapping of keys is distracting and discourteous. If you need to type something or use the computer whilst your client is on the phone explain what you are doing. If you need to put the client on speaker phone for any reason let the client know what you are doing – again it is discourteous to do so without explaining first.

TELEPHONE RAGE

Whatever you do, **do not** get angry with other people on the telephone. Find ways to deal with your irritation. One partner would simply put the phone down when he felt his blood pressure rising, wait a few minutes, dial the other person and then say sweetly, 'I'm terribly sorry about that, we've been having real problems with the office phones today.' Another would look sorrowfully at his trainee and bang his head with his knuckles while mouthing 'He's a very silly man' or even 'a very, very silly man'. It's much better to say 'I'll have to get back to you on that one,' than to engage in a telephonic shouting match. Shouting is not being assertive; it's just plain rude, and is a sign that you are not in control.

Patience works

Be patient with clients on the telephone, especially foreign ones. Try to guide them, but also leave them space to tell you what they want. One Chinese client came to a firm in order to purchase first one flat and then another in a prestigious London development; he stayed with the firm and gave a whole string of small matters relating to these flats to the firm.

The only difficulty was that he was unable to get to the point of the moment without starting at the beginning of the transaction. If he was interrupted he would simply start at the beginning again. As time passed it could take a 15-minute recitation before the point of the call was reached. But the trainee who was assigned to deal with the client listened very patiently and retained a client who subsequently recommended more clients to the firm.

As a trainee you may well find you are yourself dealing with other people's frustrations on the telephone. 'I'm not taking this call,' says your supervisor to switchboard, 'put him through to my trainee' – this is one way that your supervisor can deal with an unwelcome caller, putting the onus on you to find out what the caller wants and to take an accurate record. Unfair though this may seem it's best to see your role as being part of a team that will get the right result in the end. After all, a client will more readily accept that your supervisor is not in the office at that moment than that he has not got round to drawing up the heads of agreement that he promised for that morning.

PERSONAL CALLS

No reasonable person would expect you not to make or take social calls on your office phone, although you may well find yourself sharing a room with someone who is not reasonable. Social calls should however be brief and to the point, a short confirmation of arrangements for that evening or a checking of diaries to arrange a meeting at the weekend rather than a half-hour discussion on the merits of West Ham's new striker or the latest Booker Prize winner.

It's also sensible to make personal calls, and if possible to take them, when you are in the room on your own, so that you have half a chance of keeping your personal affairs to yourself. Keep your personal mobile turned off or in silent mode when you are in the office, and don't think that the quiet tapping of a text message won't irritate the person that you are sharing office space with.

UNEQUAL STATUS

You have a telephone on your desk, but how you can use it will usually be dictated by the person with whom you share a room. Trainees have been told:

- Do not make or take social calls during working hours.
- I shall be thinking this afternoon, so I want you to be quiet. Don't make any calls, don't take any calls, ask switchboard to route them to your secretary. Even client calls? Even client calls.
- Don't make or take any calls whatsoever while I am in the room.
- I don't like other people phoning in my room, so that's why you don't have a telephone. If you need to phone anyone, use your secretary's one or find a meeting room.

The first restriction is just about reasonable, because you are there to work and not to chat to your friends, but the others are not. Unfortunately there is very little that you can do when someone more senior exercises his proprietorial rights in this way. Except to make the resolution that on qualification you will NOT choose to work for this particular fee-earner.

Do not for a moment imagine that any ban on social calls will be reciprocated. Having just told your mother that you cannot speak to her now and that you will have to call her after work, you may then be treated for the next hour to a succession of calls detailing your supervisor's love life, social arrangements and dissatisfaction with his bank manager.

EMAILS

Fortunately you can use emails to get round the no social calls dilemma, unless of course the partner you are sitting with objects to your typing. However, at least you can read emails without making too much noise and stop and start typing them as and when your supervisor leaves the room.

Your firm may well have a written email policy. Even if it doesn't, common sense dictates that you should not:

- Copy more people into an email than is absolutely necessary. If you do, people will stop reading your emails because they will see your name in their inbox and assume that it is another irrelevant cc.
- Copy or forward confidential emails. All confidential information should be treated on a 'need to know' basis.
- Use email when you could just as easily or more politely speak to the person instead. Good working relations are easier to build or sustain if there is face-to-face as well as distance communication.
- Use mail to get angry or get even. Do not capitalise words in an email unless it is clear that you are not SHOUTING. In email etiquette capitalising something usually means shouting. Underline or italicise instead for emphasis; this is less aggressive. If you are angry when you type an email, put it in your drafts folder, leave it for ten minutes and then reread it before you send it. You may be surprised at what you have written.
- Make your emails too long. If they go on for more than a screen, ask yourself if they should be in hard copy or sent as an attachment instead.
- Forget that your secretary has access to your email. She needs access to be able to remind you of appointments and pending issues and deadlines. This does mean, on the other hand, that she can read what you have to say about your personal life and your opinions of other people whether in or out of the office.

On the other hand, do:

- Answer your emails promptly. In recent years clients have come to expect that solicitors will have virtually instant access to emails through handheld devices and will reply almost instantaneously. As some firms expect holding responses to be sent within hours, check your office manual for what is expected of you. Unless you are away (in which case your out-of-office reply must be on) clients and supervisors will anticipate that you will reply within a day.
- Be just as careful with your spelling and expression in an email to a client or to a senior colleague as you would be with a formal letter or a research note. Shoddy work in any guise leaves a bad impression. Use the email spell checker.

- Regularly delete unwanted emails as otherwise your mailbox could become so full that clients, members of your firm or anyone else who is trying to communicate with you will find that your mailbox is closed and will get a message telling them so. If you get a message telling you that your mailbox is reaching capacity take immediate action. Having a full mailbox makes you look sloppy. Before you go on holiday clear out sufficient space so that your mailbox does not fill up while you are away and set up an automated out-of-office message. In it you should indicate your dates of absence and who should be contacted if a matter is urgent. Usually this will be your secretary but check first before you use your secretary's details in your message.
- Keep personal emails as 'clean' as possible; smutty jokes may be alright with your friends in the bar but could amount to a serious breach of the firm's equality and diversity policy.
- Remember that anyone in the firm can obtain access to your email. So, keep bitchy, complaining comments about your irritating partner/incompetent secretary/the Senior Partner's dreadful dress sense to yourself, and at least don't put them in written form.
- Make sure that you never, ever swear on email. You could inadvertently send it to the wrong person or your email could be required for some perfectly legitimate purpose in the future where your blast of expletives could be at best embarrassing or at worst actionable.
- Curb any tendencies you have to 'slag people off' on email, either directly to the person concerned or by way of letting off steam to another person. Emails can be printed out, forwarded, copied or retrieved and could come back to haunt you either by being a clog on your promotion or by dragging you into court.

EASY-TO-MAKE EMAIL ERRORS

Be aware of the dangers of pressing 'reply all' when you want your smart-Alec comments to go to only one person. One trainee invited almost everyone he knew to his leaving drinks, including clients and people he had worked with from other firms. Unfortunately when replying to the email invitation one of his friends pressed the 'Reply All' button, with a question about whether some sort of double action was required.

If you do send an email with a large circulation list, consider putting all the recipients in the BCC (blind copy) box and send the email to yourself. This will mean that the recipients don't see all the other email addresses and there is no risk of an accidental 'Reply All'.

Make sure that you are replying to the correct email. In your haste to deal with an avalanche of emails it is easy to send a reply to your friend explaining that 'I can't see you this evening because that overbearing freak client, Mr Bustard, has left everything to the last minute again. Can't wait to move on to the next seat to get shot of him,' but to realise later that you have sent it to Mr Bustard, whose instruction email just happened to be underneath the one from your friend. This is when you start to ask yourself who is more important to the firm, you or Mr Bustard...

Chapter 14

YOUR PLACE IN THE OFFICE

SPEED READ SUMMARY

■ Firms and trainees often have very different ideas of trainees' immediate value to their firm. Firms often view trainees as an expensive overhead while trainees view themselves as an excellent source of revenue.

■ Because the costs of inadequate or negligent work are potentially so large in terms of lost clients, reputation and *in extremis* being sued, good firms expend a substantial amount of money and time in ensuring that trainees don't make mistakes.

■ If you do make a mistake you should own up to it immediately. The longer it takes to admit mistakes the worse the consequences can be for the client, for your firm and for you. Just in case, you should have some strategies for admission and rectification already worked out.

■ Sharing a room with someone for up to ten hours a day can be very difficult and you need to remember that you are the 'junior' occupant.

■ It is your responsibility to ensure that you get enough work to do.

DO YOU DESERVE YOUR SALARY?

Trainees are employees and have to be useful at some level. Just how that usefulness is perceived depends on whether you are a trainee or a partner. What the trainee sees is the hourly rate that the firm charges for the trainee's services, the number of hours spent on a matter, the sum of the hours by the charging rate and possibly the ultimate bill, if the trainee is asked to prepare a draft 'narrative' to go out for what will now seem like a horrendous amount of money. It's easy to feel that you have 'earned your annual salary' by Christmas because of the numbers that have been going down on the time sheet, and even to feel that the salary that seemed so vast in October is simply not enough for your heroic efforts.

Before you get too pleased with yourself, remember that the money that you have 'earned' has to help to pay a small part of the firm's overheads, the salaries of the secretaries, the rent on the office, the coffee and biscuits in the morning, the new computer on your desk and the engineer at the end of the phone who puts things right. Etc, etc, etc.

From the partners' point of view you are an untested 'human resource' that needs to be brought up to speed. The faster that you can reach this state, then the sooner that you can start to make real money for the firm. Many firms consider that not only are trainees a drain on the firm's finances for the whole of their training contract but that they do not make any real money for the firm until they have been qualified for at least a year and probably two.

THE COST OF MISTAKES

Much of this difference in perception is down to the different attitudes to making mistakes, which you and your employers will probably have at this stage in your career.

'Everybody makes mistakes.' Yes, that's true, and it is what the legal profession thrives on, the desire by others to prevent future disputes or misunderstandings or the wish to have them rectified as soon as possible. But clients do not want 75% (Grade A) leases or 60% (Grade B) Employee Share Plans. They want triple-starred Firsts for every piece of work that you do for them.

It follows therefore that firms cannot afford to let you cut your teeth by making unsupervised mistakes. Therefore every piece of work should initially be looked over by your supervisor, and only gradually should the reins of supervision be loosened. You should not get uptight about this, and you should recognise that this all takes time.

Remember that one of a law firm's most consistent overheads is the cost of insurance, and that a proportion of this will be computed on its previous claims record in the same way that your car insurance is. At various points in the year fee-earners are asked to fill in forms stating whether they know of any matter in which they are involved which is likely to give rise to a claim. The assumption is that the answer will be in the negative, but the purpose is to make fee-earners ask themselves whether they are handling any files where things are, or might be, going wrong.

DON'T HIDE MISTAKES

If you think that you have made a mistake, own up to it. Don't try to conceal it, and certainly don't do this at the end of your seat, when you are handing the file on to another trainee. If something is wrong it will be found out at some point or other, and if it is traced back to you, you will be seen as incompetent, negligent or as someone who is not to be trusted to look out for his own colleagues. No one likes to be 'dumped in it' and hoping that your supervisor or a subsequent trainee will take the blame for your mistake is not just unfair, but stupid. Remember that law firms are villages, and that lawyers have long memories – that is one of their skills. You will often find that antipathies between partners can be traced back to some incident in the distant past when they were both trainees.

The chances are that your 'mistake' will not have been serious or even real, but was simply a misapprehension of the law or procedure. If you own up, you can either be reassured or the mistake can be rectified. You may not find it very gratifying to listen to your supervisor explaining to a client that 'My trainee uncharacteristically sent out an incomplete draft of that lease that you needed. I'll have the complete draft couriered round to you by the end of the day, so please would you destroy the draft that you have now and please accept my apologies.' Hold on to the word 'uncharacteristically'. And remember that this is much better than your having kept silent, your supervisor finding out by himself and the client having wasted an hour or so reading through the wrong draft. With any luck you may get the opportunity to apologise to the client and to allow yourself to be teased about it. Good client/solicitor relationships can often be built on seemingly unpromising foundations.

Even if your supervisor is of the unforgiving sort, it is still good policy to own up. The deeper that your supervisor gets in the mire before the mistake is discovered, the deeper hole you will have dug for yourself. If it gets so bad that he has to make a special trip to discuss your error with the Managing Partner this will suggest inadequate supervision on his part, and will almost certainly have implications for his report on your work and your future in the firm.

HOW TO OWN UP

There are various approaches here, depending on your assessment of your supervisor's character. Whatever you do, try to choose as propitious a moment as possible, and if at all possible choose a time when you are not likely to be interrupted. If you know that your supervisor needs three cups of coffee in the morning to get up to speed, then even if you have spent half the night worrying about whether you should have told the client at eight pm the previous evening that there would be no VAT to pay on the very expensive sapphire and diamond ring he was planning to bring back from Bangkok in two weeks' time for his girlfriend, wait until the requisite amount of caffeine has been consumed before you blurt out your incompetence.

If it is a question of legal fact or interpretation, you could start by framing a general question: 'I've been wondering if it's the case that... ' Then if you get the answer you want, there is no need to go any further. But if the answer conflicts with the advice that you gave the client, then is the time to admit that you have given it.

Don't make a song and dance about how you have not slept all night, but ask for advice on what you can do to retrieve the situation. It may be possible that you will be permitted to sort out the error by yourself. 'Phone him up and say that you have thought about his question again, and consulted me and explain what the true position is and why.' Clients like to feel that you are constantly thinking about them and their problems and will appreciate that you have taken the time to correct any misinformation. Immediately.

If you get off lightly with your supervisor, then say 'thank you'. If you don't get off lightly, then apologise once more, and leave it at that. Don't grovel. Being wrong is bad enough but being wrong and having no self-respect is infinitely worse.

Burying bad news

Don't ever try to 'bury' your mistakes. They won't just magically disappear; indeed the consequences will multiply like a rapidly expanding rash. John, a recently qualified solicitor, made the mistake on completion of a sale for a client of sending all the proceeds of sale of a residential property to the client without arranging for the mortgage redemption monies to be sent to the bank. He 'sort of' realised what he had done, but instead of admitting his error to the partner in charge he put the file back in the cupboard.

If he had immediately admitted his error, the partner would have been able to explain the error to the firm's bank and arranged for the money transfer to be stopped and the funds reallocated. Instead, the partner discovered the error a week later when the bank would not release a redemption certificate to the purchaser's solicitor.

What happened next:
- The vendor client had gone on a long holiday and was apparently ignoring letters asking for the excess funds to be reimbursed. John's firm then went to court to obtain a freezing order on the client's assets.
- John's firm had to report his error to its insurers and spend time writing reports. There was the possibility that as a result of his action the firm's insurance premiums would go up.
- As the firm was a small one, the time spent on dealing with this and the potentially increased premiums could have made a serious difference to its profitability that year. There was certainly damage to the firm's relationship with the client, the bank and the solicitors on the other side.

And John? He was immediately suspended and his firm ultimately decided that they could not continue to employ someone who had breached their trust.

SORT IT OUT

Some supervisors will be susceptible to a trainee's lip quivering and tears. However, it's not really the impression that you want to leave someone with, that you are going to degenerate into nineteenth-century Jane Austen vapours at the first sign of difficulty. You might do this only once, but it may well be remembered.

If you know that you are going to find it difficult to explain what you have done, or what has concerned you, then write a note and ask your supervisor to read it, say where you are going to be for the next 15 minutes and then leave the room. Curiosity will probably get the note read and your supervisor will have had the opportunity to calm down by the time that you come back. Or simply to have had a chuckle because the horrendous mistake that you made was not a mistake at all, or one of very minimal consequence.

But this can be a risky strategy. Lawyers live in a world where pieces of paper are filed. Your confession, even if it has a scrawled 'Said it was OK' at the bottom, may well end up in the file of the matter that you were worried about, for other people to see.

What you must never, ever do, is to try to bury your mistake and hope that it will not be found. Suppose that you did not check the VAT position of the jewellery importation with your supervisor, and the client, who thought that he would buy a sapphire bracelet as well as the ring, was shocked to find that he not only had to pay VAT at 17.5% but duty too on his gifts... We leave the rest to your imagination.

SHARING A ROOM

Sharing a room with someone (or sharing space if your office is open plan) for six months or longer can be difficult. Why do you think that most murders take place within families? Little idiosyncrasies that can be laughed about over a short period of time are magnified if they are repeated several times a day over a long period of time.

It can be very exciting to be allocated your first desk, with its own PC, its own dictation machine, your own telephone, pens, pads and so on. Instead of the search for a bit of study space in the university or law college library, you now have half a room (or at least your very own workstation) to call your own.

Yet another difference of perception

Your 'ownership' of office space is nominal and it would be wise to remember that you are only a temporary bird of passage. In every room or open-plan floor there is a dominant fee-earner. This is the case whether the office space is being shared by two assistants or a partner and an assistant. And it is certainly true where one of the fee-earners is a trainee.

The dominant-servient relationship (to borrow a term from Land Law) is usually dictated by seniority, often by the intensity of the pressure to perform in financial terms, but also by the personality of the dominant fee-earner. The atmosphere in different rooms or on different floors, even in the same department, can be radically different.

The pressures on you as a trainee are threefold: to learn as much as you can, to make as few mistakes as you can and to earn as much as you can for the firm. It will be assumed that the person with whom you are sitting already knows a lot and does not often make mistakes (although if mistakes are made, they can be huge) so that the pressure on your supervisor is to earn as much as possible. Put crudely, your supervisor's time is simply more potentially lucrative than yours and that gives a greater entitlement to space, whether physical or emotional. It is also likely that although you will share the same secretary, your supervisor's entitlement to her time will take priority.

> ## Getting onside
>
> Sometimes it can help to make the first move with superiors who are difficult to please.
> Try asking them out for lunch and for feedback on how you could make the most of your seat.
>
> Listen attentively and don't argue back. You might learn something helpful and you don't have to adhere to all their suggestions.

So try to be tidy, and to keep your work space, floor space and files separate from your supervisor's. But don't assume that the more senior lawyer will accord you the same courtesy. Some solicitors are excessively tidy to the point of lining up their work in regimented, matching plastic folders on their desks at the end of the day so that they present themselves eagerly at the ready for each new day. Even the plants on the window sill, if there are any, will have to stand up straight. In the view of such a person your untidy desk simply indicates that you have an untidy mind.

Other solicitors operate on desks cascading with paper arranged in no particular order of importance; when they need a space to work on, they simply move some of the paper onto the nearest available space. Curiously they often know exactly what is on their desks and where to find what they want. They clearly will not castigate you for being untidy, but it is even more important that you keep control of your own work and papers in this type of office. You do not want the freshly sworn affidavit returned from the client who has just boarded a plane to Los Angeles to disappear under one of your supervisor's miscellaneous files.

However gruff or senior the person you are sharing with, try to ascertain politely when you first move into the room what cupboard space you can have and where your files should be kept. Some partners are considerate and will keep a shelf or two in their room for the 'trainee files', but in other cases you will just have to file on the floor. The most important thing is to adopt the ethos of the room as far as possible, although in most cases it is best to err on the side of tidiness and confidentiality. The data in the files need to be kept securely and this usually means being filed away in a lockable filing cabinet.

In your first seat at least you should anticipate that most of the work that you do will originate with your supervisor, which means that in effect you will be sharing files and clients. This of course does bring its own problems, because your supervisor may suddenly want to refresh his memory on something contained in the file when you are in the middle of examining a complex lease provision. Mark where you've got to, and hand it over. 'In a minute' does not cut it here.

Territoriality and idiosyncrasies

Some lawyers are very idiosyncratic and however quirky they are you will simply have to accept many of their oddities: the compulsive shining of the shoes before a meeting with clients; the loud crunching of apples at precisely 11.30 and 3.30 every day; the pulling down of the office blinds every time that 'thinking time' is required; the demand that a trainee work through his lunch hour with the accompanying injunction that 'if you are going to eat crisps in my office, you must suck them'. These are relatively amusing and easy to tolerate because your sojourn in that room will be for a brief period of time. But some things are harder to handle.

One partner breezed into work on his motorbike every day, strode straight to his office, got out of his leathers and proceeded to change into his shirt and suit. This was strange but marginally acceptable as long as he had male trainees. His first female trainee was told about this likely performance by his previous trainees who were eager to see how she would react. So what did she do? She could have complained to HR. But she took the pragmatic decision that it was after all his office, and simply ensured that when he arrived she had something to look up in the library and disappeared for 15 minutes leaving him to himself.

It was relatively easy for this particular trainee to take this pragmatic attitude because the partner's behaviour, although thoughtless, would have had no sexual intention behind it. It was simply the quickest way that he had worked out to get himself from home to operational status every morning, and the trainee realised that this was the case.

Sexual harassment or bullying should be treated differently. It's easy to say this, but it can be very difficult to handle because the person who is harassing or bullying is inevitably, or appears to be, in a position to influence your career. But you should be careful that what you are experiencing really is harassment or bullying and not merely thoughtless behaviour which you might be able to accept, ignore or deal with without getting the whole office involved. (See Chapter 17.)

Dealing with unhappiness

Whether or not you are enjoying a seat you owe it to yourself to apply yourself, as the effort that you are seen to make in any particular department will have an impact on the wider firm's view of you. Even if you know that you do not want to qualify into that particular seat, the work that you are given seems like make-weight trainee fodder (files that are handed on from one trainee to the next over a long period because your supervisor knows that it is not urgent as far as the client is concerned and the fees will not compensate for the time expended) and you would much rather spend time learning more about the work of the department that you do want to qualify into, still – make that effort!

You never know what will impress. One trainee, bored out of his mind doing petty debt-collecting in the Litigation department earned a glowing report simply because of a phone conversation with a threatening debtor, who had attempted to intimidate him. What the supervisor had picked up was coolness and courtesy and not the fact that that particular trainee was counting off the days until his release from the department.

Oddities

In reality you will not encounter all or even any of the difficulties listed below, but you will not be alone if you share a room with someone who:

- has apparently taken a bath in neat, cheap eau de cologne
- puts half-eaten pies in the bottom drawer of his desk along with old shoes and paper clips
- scrupulously locks up everything in sight when he leaves his room and has no personal effects visible in the room (male lawyers particularly usually have photographs of their children prominently on display) 'just in case it gives too much away'
- throws a squash ball repeatedly against the wall when thinking
- insists that the room be illuminated only by desk lamps. Try looking for

files or books in a darkened cupboard; your supervisor will simply call in his secretary to find them.

■ cycles to work and then dries sweaty cycle gear on the radiator

In contrast you should aim to be as innocuous as possible. You must not create a visual, auditory or olfactory nuisance.

Silence please

If you share a room with a relatively senior partner, and particularly with someone who is a Head of Department, you may well be asked to leave the room at frequent intervals. There is absolutely nothing you can object to in this, because the matters that are being discussed, either on the phone or in person with another partner, are often confidential and potentially highly sensitive, whether it is just one partner mouthing off to the other about a third partner or whether it is a discussion about salary increases or possible redundancies. But don't just treat this as 'free time' when you can wander round the office or go off for a cup of coffee. You should always have something at the ready that you can take off to the library or a quiet place to get on with. If you do not, you may well find that you are having to spend out-of-office hours just to keep up with your workload.

One senior partner however said to a newly qualified assistant who was about to share his room, 'I've got work to do and you've got work to do, and you can't be leaving the room every time that someone comes in to speak to me. I'm going to trust you to keep your mouth shut about everything that you hear. But, and I mean this, if I find that you have been passing on anything that you have overheard in this room, then you will not have a pleasant time in this firm.'

That was clear and to the point, and fair. And hard as it was, the assistant did succeed in keeping his mouth shut.

GETTING WORK

If you are in a new seat and your supervisor does not provide you with anything to do after a few days (and this does happen) then ask if there is anything that you can do to help.

There may in reality be no work to give you. This could be because all the matters your supervisor is working on are too complex, your supervisor is not very good at delegating and resents being asked to do so or perhaps there is simply not enough work to go round. In the latter case your supervisor is not going to pass anything over to you that could possibly go down on his own time sheet as a benefit to his billing targets and therefore career. This is where you are going to have to show some initiative.

First, double check that there is really nothing that you can be given. Then ask if it is alright if you ask other fee-earners in the department if they have any work for you. This will either galvanise your supervisor into delegation or you will be out there 'foraging'. Going to ask fee-earners whom you barely know if they have any work for you may seem an odd start to your legal career, but try to think of it positively. It shows enthusiasm on your part, gets your face known and could result in a greater variety of work than if you spend your whole six months' seat working on one big case that has not come to a conclusion by the time that you move on to the next seat.

This is one situation where you really must be proactive. If the worst comes to the worst, use your time to get to grips with required legal reading for your current department, even ask if you can do a note for the department on an important case which is crucial for their work. Whatever you do, don't spend your time chatting to other trainees in the corridors, phoning your friends to get the latest gossip or playing internet poker.

Chapter 15

KEEPING HEALTHY

SPEED READ SUMMARY

■ Your ability to stay healthy will affect your ability to work well and efficiently.

■ Eating sensibly will maximise your ability to perform.

■ Taking exercise will improve your stamina.

■ Drinking immoderately will make you sluggish and diminish your effectiveness.

■ Spending too much can be just as addictive as alcohol.

HARD-WORK CITY

Being a lawyer can be hard work, very hard work indeed. If you are ill or under the weather your underperformance will affect your colleagues and your clients as well as yourself. Unfair or not, your ability to remain healthy and turn up to work every day could form part of the decision as to whether you should be kept on at the end of your training contract.

If you want to move jobs, one of the first things that your new or prospective employer will ask for is your sick leave record.

There are three key things that you should pay particular attention to – exercise, food and alcohol.

Trainees with a disability

If you have a disability this chapter also applies, but clearly your firm has obligations to make it possible for you to work to the best of your ability, including making reasonable adjustments such as alternative work arrangements so that you can work from home some of the time.

EXERCISE

Juvenal was certainly right when he spoke about the importance of *mens sana in corpore sano*, or a healthy mind in a healthy body. Taking exercise will improve the blood flow to the brain, will rest the brain, will enable you to sit upright at your desk (remember that many back problems are caused through the weakening of back and stomach muscles caused by long hours sitting at a desk), will improve your immunity to the general colds and flu that are fostered in an office environment in the winter and also your chances of going on holiday without being in a state of total exhaustion. If you choose a form of exercise that you enjoy, it will reduce your stress levels.

After university and even law school where you might have been able to take exercise on a whim, it may now seem all too difficult. 'I'm thinking about going for a swim after work,' or 'If I get this lease finished I might go to the gym,' too often gets translated into 'Yes, I'll go for a drink, I'll swim tomorrow,' and 'I've finished the lease now, but it's too late to go to the gym.'

There really is only one way to deal with this if you are an exercise ditherer and that is to slot exercise 'appointments' into your diary. Not only will you be encouraged to 'attend' them, but your routines will gradually register with other people. Your secretary will know not to make appointments for you at those times without consulting you first, and other people's assumptions that you will not be available will force you to remove yourself from your desk.

As a trainee you will not have the same control over your diary as you will have later, but you should start now to think about how you want your future life in a legal office to shape up. Building in some sort of exercise, even if it is just changing your work shoes for cross-trainers and walking briskly round a few city streets at lunchtime, will help you to maintain longevity and pleasure in what you do. Exercise does not have to be taken in gruelling two-hour sessions; as the supermarket ad says 'Every little helps.' Aim to fit in at least three 20-minute sessions a week and before starting an exercise regime take advice from a suitably qualified person (you can tell that lawyers wrote this book, can't you?).

Making exercise work

Find a time of day that works for you and a form of exercise that works for you. Look around and you will find a multitude of ways in which your colleagues have solved the exercise conundrum for themselves. In one large office you might find:

- Two colleagues who have a game of squash at eight am two mornings a week before getting to work
- Someone who swims three days a week before work, arriving perhaps 15–20 minutes late but then making up the time at the end of the day
- Someone who takes an additional 15 minutes at lunchtime so that she can change into running gear and run round the park
- Someone who puts in a very brisk and intensive half hour at the gym at 5.30 three days a week before coming back to the office to carry on working
- Someone who takes tango classes twice a week
- Someone who cycles to work four mornings a week. On the fifth day clean work clothes for the following week are brought in and the previous week's 'dirties' are taken home. Of course this requires a bit of organisation and planning, but then that is one of the skills that lawyers should acquire.

Your firm's involvement

Some larger firms actively encourage their staff to exercise. The facilities they provide in the way of swimming pools, gyms and dedicated gym personnel would put some health clubs to shame. Use them. If your firm indicates that it wants to keep you healthy by putting in these facilities, take it at its word. The firm does not provide them out of pure benevolence, but because the partners realise that people like the idea of working in organisations which provide gyms and swimming pools and that people who take exercise are more likely to be able to cope with stress. Many firms also provide their fee-earners with full-blown annual medicals, because they have a vested interest in their solicitors staying healthy.

Other firms which cannot afford the plush provision of the major City firms may encourage their staff to form softball teams, netball teams, cricket and football teams, partly for bonding and team-building but also as a way of encouraging them to take exercise. Even in a very small firm it may be possible to get enough people interested to form a team to play against other teams in your area. Getting motivated to take exercise is often a lot easier if you have an exercise buddy or you are a part of a team.

One of the mistakes that trainees make is to feel that they have to give up all other interests to devote themselves entirely to their new careers. The law is demanding and often fascinating, which makes it easy to decide that it is all too difficult to carry on playing rugby or golf at the weekend or to go for the odd weekend's fell-walking which has been a regular part of your life up till now. This is a very bad mistake, not only because you will be lacking the vital exercise that you need, but because it will cut you off from what is you – your previous life outside the office.

FOOD

When you are working hard it is easy to carry on working at your desk at lunchtime, munching a sandwich, or worse still a couple of bars of chocolate, while you carry on working in the belief that you are saving time and will get the job done faster. While this probably will not do you too much harm on an occasional basis it is not a sensible long-term strategy. It's far better to:

- Go to the firm's canteen where you can rest your brain, which is after all just another muscle that can get very tired indeed, by speaking to colleagues about things that have nothing to do with the law, or at least nothing to do with your particular matter.
- Find a quiet place to eat your sandwich outside the office. Even large cities have churchyards and small parks where you can sit and eat in peace.
- Go for a brisk walk and then come back to eat your sandwich. Remember that to function properly human beings need light and the Vitamin D that they get from sunlight.
- Take some more active exercise. Go for a very brisk walk, go to the gym, go for a run, play squash with a colleague or go for a swim.

Towards a sensible diet

Now really is the time to try to give up on junk food, and to try to eat a balanced diet. You are embarking on a life much of which will be spent behind a desk for long periods of time and your body may simply not be able to process the amount of fat and carbohydrate that it was able to do when you were at school and university. Keeping to a healthy eating regime can be very difficult because trainee social life is often centred around drinking after work followed by eating at cheap restaurants that serve pasta, pizza and curries. This makes it even more important that you follow some sort of exercise plan to enable your body to cope.

In most offices coffee and tea are very freely available – and free. It is easy to treat a visit to the coffee machine as a sensible break from your desk between pieces of work, or to use tea, coffee and cola as stimulants to keep you going if you have to work late. As you probably know from late-night revision sessions at university this can be very effective, but can also mean that your energy levels crash later. Remember that intense caffeine consumption for exams is short term, but that you are going to be in the office for upwards of 45 weeks a year. You cannot live in 'two weeks before Finals' mode for the whole of your working life – or at least you will pay for it if you try to do so.

Different people have different levels of tolerance to caffeine. It is a good idea to monitor how much you take and to see if you can cut down. If you are sleeping badly or waking in the morning feeling unrefreshed, ask yourself whether this is caused by drinking too much coffee or cola in the afternoon or evening.

There is a great deal of information about the bad effects of smoking on various aspects of your long- and short-term health, but did you know that if you smoke, the coffee that you drink provides you with less of a 'lift' so that you will most likely end up consuming more caffeine than you otherwise would with potentially even more bad effects on your health?

You will inevitably find that you will need some sort of snack to keep you going on the days when work interferes with normal lunch or leaving times. Eating fruit or compressed fruit bars to stave off hunger pangs is preferable to munching chocolate and biscuits. Keep a supply of dry, healthy snacks in your desk drawer.

ENTERTAINING LUNCHES

At client lunches and lunchtime seminars choose the 'healthy option' if there is one and drink water even if everyone else is drinking wine. If you do drink wine, make sure that you are also drinking water. And never, ever drink wine if everyone else is drinking water. If you are teased about passing up alcohol, you can say that you have a lot of work to get on with later or alternatively blame it on your metabolism and say that you cannot eat a lot or drink at lunchtime without falling asleep: 'I must have been a big cat in my previous existence.' After a while people will simply take this for granted. Your lunch companions may even be relieved since it takes the pressure off them to drink at lunchtime simply to be 'polite'.

Never order dessert unless someone senior chooses to. People are busy and don't want to be kept hanging around waiting for you to finish your crème brûlée.

SOCIAL DRINKING

In common with many other organisations, much of legal socialising centres round alcohol. Colleagues go out together after work, partners entertain their staff, lawyers take clients out to lunch or dinner, events are organised for client entertainment which inevitably feature 'refreshments' and even sporting events end up in the pub afterwards. From being in a university environment where drinking is desirable but not readily affordable you may now find yourself in one where you are actively being encouraged to drink as part of your working life.

If you attend client events, are taken out to lunch or dinner with clients, attend staff social events out of the office or play in a sports event after work you will find that the firm picks up most, if not all, of the tab. It can seem like a free-loader's paradise. But beware – your liver, your general health, mental as well as physical, and your professional competence are under attack.

REALITY CHECK

Take a look at the website of *LawCare*, an organisation which provides health support and advice for lawyers. They point out that 30% of male lawyers and 20% of female lawyers regularly exceed the recommended drinking levels and up to 15% become addicted. Alcohol-related deaths in the legal profession are seriously high with lawyers suffering double the national death rate from cirrhosis of the liver.

Even highly successful lawyers have been asked to leave their partnerships because their alcohol-fuelled behaviour has become an embarrassment to their fellow partners. If you realise that now, you should have a better chance of avoiding that difficulty.

This is not to suggest that you should not avail yourself of the hospitality on offer, share some down-time and a drink with colleagues, but that you should learn to pace yourself both in terms of how many times you drink in a week and how much you drink at a time. If you buy better wine you might find that you actually drink less, not just because of the price, but because you will need less as you are drinking to savour it rather than for the alcoholic effect.

If you feel that you are running into difficulties with alcohol or indeed with any other addictive substance you will find a list at the end of the book of organisations accustomed to helping legal professionals in trouble.

Drinking buddies

Bear in mind that it is possible to make a complete fool of yourself at a client function because you have failed to monitor your alcohol intake, particularly if you attend on an empty stomach. Put some strategies in place to avoid this. Agree with one of your colleagues that you will find each other for an 'appraisal meeting' by the door at specific times during the function. You should agree beforehand that:

■ If your colleague thinks that you have had too much to drink or are on the point of doing so, then you must leave without demur
■ If you really are in a bad way, your colleague must get you out of the building and into a taxi as soon as possible

This buddy system can be equally useful at office parties, another potential place for career suicide.

THE MATERIAL ALTERNATIVE

Another version of the Friday night post-work binge is another modern 'sport'. As one young lawyer put it, 'at the end of a hard week in the office, I just go out to the shops, and I spend just for the pleasure of spending what I've earned that week. It doesn't really matter what I buy as long as I buy something.'

Before you blow all your hard-earned cash on things that you do not need, take a closer look at your behaviour. For a long time you may have had to deny yourself the pleasure, and it is one, of being able to buy something on a whim without doing the 'one textbook equals seven pints of beer or seventeen cans of beans' computation. Now that you have a regular salary you can so easily fall prey to materialism addiction, a temptation that is enhanced in many offices by the fact that you are dealing with transactions involving large amounts of money.

Remember that you do not need to emulate your clients in money terms or anything else. You would not feel that you needed to ape a fraudster because you defended him, so you should not allow yourself to spend money that you have worked hard to earn just because you happen to be acting for a millionaire to whom your salary would be of no consequence. It's very important at this point in your career to hold on to what you consider to be your core values and to maintain your own standards. If indulging in regular happy-go-lucky spending sprees and expensive holidays is what you really enjoy, then although that may produce long-term difficulties, that is your decision. But make sure that it is your decision and not just a short-term fix or 'rush' because you are too tired to do anything more constructive or because spending money is an antidote to feeling miserable in some aspect of your life.

Chapter 16

FINANCES

SPEED READ SUMMARY

■ Budgeting is important because expenditure can so easily expand to cover all the cash you have available.

■ Before you start work, try to estimate the cost of all the essentials in your new life. Allow for student loan repayments and estimate how much you might be able to set aside for savings and pensions.

■ Use store cards and credit cards prudently, so that your salary is not depleted by unnecessary interest payments.

■ Be meticulous with record-keeping. Treat yourself as a client.

THE FINANCIAL PICTURE

After life as a student the salary which you will now be receiving may seem when offered to you like riches beyond comprehension. If you are working for a large City firm, the equally large numbers before the zeros coupled with the very public repetition in the press of the salaries of senior City partners may lull you into a very false sense of financial security. Remember that expenditure expands according to the cash available and, if you are not careful, to just beyond the cash available. For some very senior lawyers their large and, to the outsider, impossible salaries do not bring personal freedom. They get caught in a money trap where their large mortgage commitments, school fees and possibly maintenance payments for ex-spouses make reading their monthly bank statements a miserable experience. Some of them probably need this financial goad to keep them at work, but they suffer not from the tyranny of choice but the misery of no choice. Getting trapped by a need to keep earning more and more money is a route to real misery. To avoid this, take control of your finances now. If you think that you do not have time to do so – make time!

It is essential that you sit down and work out what your outgoings are likely to be. There are obvious things like rent, food and transport. City salaries particularly appear vast but the cost of a roof over your head and getting to work can be much more substantial than you may have anticipated. When you are doing a budget remember to factor in the increased cost of better clothing and footwear for work and the cost of better haircuts and dry cleaning.

Try to assess your necessary outgoings before you start work, when the memory of how little you can survive on is still fresh in your mind. This is not an invitation to be a skinflint or a miser, merely to be aware about what your salary can and can't do for you. If you know how much is coming in and going out each month you are less likely to succumb to the pressure from friends or a partner to spend money you haven't got: 'Come on, of course we can afford an exotic holiday – look how much you are on now!' or 'Don't be daft – you earn enough to get those sofas.' Don't get carried away with the thought of spending all that you earn – and more.

STUDENT LOAN REPAYMENTS

Even in smaller law firms your salary will be such that there will be an automatic deduction from your salary to start paying off your student loan as soon as you start working. Because the deductions are calculated on a percentage of your salary above a threshold level (currently £15,000) this is the amount that you will automatically have to pay. It follows therefore that if your salary is higher your loan will be paid off more quickly, but working in a smaller practice may mean that your student loan is hanging over your head for some time. Try to take a time-bounded view of this. Consider what your outgoings are and work out whether you could pay it all back over a shorter period. Then try to stick with your plan. That is much better than saying airily 'I'll pay back chunks of it when I can,' because you can always find other things to do with your money and 'when you can' may never come. If you set up automatic deductions to a savings account you will hardly notice the apparent reduction in your salary after the first month or two, because you will have removed choice and therefore having to think about it.

On the other hand you may be more comfortable paying the loan off gradually because the rate of interest charged on the outstanding loan may be less than you could get in a tax-free ISA for example. The important thing is to sit down and consider carefully what will work for you and your long-term plans.

PENSIONS

You have just embarked on your professional career and 'retirement' should seem a very long way in the future. However, despite all the bad press devoted to the pensions industry over recent years, pensions saving for your retirement is the only way that you can persuade the state not only to allow you to roll up your savings tax free but also to give you some tax back at the time that you make the pension investment.

The sooner you start investing in a pension the less you will need to invest. This is because of the effect of compounding. Assuming that you retire at 65 every pound that you invest at the age of 25 will have 40 years to roll up tax free whereas a pound invested at the age of 50 will have only 15.

Although pension investment can also be more flexible than you might imagine, you should also remember that the money invested in pensions cannot be accessed until you are at least 50. You are permitted to invest all the money that you earn in a year (up to an annual limit and up to a life-time limit, neither of which generous limit you will be likely to breach for many years to come) in a personal pension plan, but the downside of this generosity is that the money cannot then be touched until you retire. It's important therefore to invest only what you can reasonably afford or not miss too much. But do not put off starting a pension just because 5% of your salary does not appear very much to start with. The increasing amount that appears each year on your annual pension statement will gradually become very gratifying indeed.

GETTING INFORMATION

Investing in a pension is a very big decision which you should research properly before you commit yourself and your money for many years ahead.

Find out what your firm's policy on pension investment is. Firms, especially the larger ones, will often donate an additional 5% of your salary to your pension fund if you yourself make a minimum investment, usually also 5%. When you make a pension contribution the taxman refunds the basic rate tax on that contribution into your pension fund. At current tax rates if you pay 5% of your after-tax salary into your pension

Regular savings

There is a Scottish proverb that says 'monie a mickle maks a muckle', which can be roughly translated as 'many small investments add up to a large one'. Saving regularly through a direct debit arrangement has the double advantage of curtailing the amount of 'free cash' that you have each month without your being too aware of it, and at the same time building up a capital sum which can be used for the down payment on a car, the deposit on a house or paying for a holiday without using a credit card.

Building societies and banks often offer higher rates of interest on regular savings plans than they do on their usual savings arrangements, because this type of account takes little time to administer once it has been set up and they have the certainty of funds coming in at a predetermined time each month. Shop around and pay attention because:

- Many banks and building societies offer higher rates of interest for the first year for this type of account, sometimes as much as 2% or even more over the normal rate.
- Some banks require you to give notice for withdrawals from this type of account, otherwise you will suffer a financial penalty.
- If you do get a high introductory rate you should make a note of the end of the higher rate investment period, and then see if you could get a better rate through another bank's regular savings plan, or indeed whether another bank would give you a higher rate for the capital that you have built up with the first bank.

fund, the taxman will refund basic rate tax of 1.25% of your salary into your fund. If your employer also contributes 5%, your pension fund will have received a total contribution of 11.25% of your salary, while you have given up the pleasure of spending only 5% of it. If you become a higher rate taxpayer you will receive an additional amount of tax relief.

Read the financial pages in the press and get information about the various pension options from a range of different pension providers.

Speak to friends who are in the investment sector and trainees or friends who specialise in pensions. You don't need to take their advice, but it will be good training for you to assess what they say and for them to try to persuade you. This is a big commitment, so it is important that you know what you are doing.

TAKING ADVICE

When you have gathered as much information as you can it might now be time to consult an independent financial adviser (IFA). Don't be afraid to ask questions and don't allow yourself to be blinded with dubious science. Don't be embarrassed to ask the IFA what he or she gets out of advising you. IFAs don't work for free. So consider how their fees are paid, as either directly or indirectly the investor will be paying.

A good IFA can suggest investments to you that you might not have considered and can save you money through giving advice that is appropriate to your circumstances. You don't have to give your business to the first one that you consult; take your time to find one that you feel comfortable with and whom you feel you could trust.

If you are thinking about investing in a pension you need to take proper financial advice about both pensions and your long-term financial strategy.

ISAs

Investing in ISAs gives you greater flexibility. ISA is an acronym for Individual Savings Account. The maximum amount that you can invest in any given year is set by the Chancellor of the Exchequer. You will obtain no tax relief on your investment going into the fund but once the money is there, any increase in value in your fund either through capital growth or income accretion will be tax free. You can invest in either or both shares and cash but only up to specified limits. The rules for cash investments are more restrictive than the rules for share investments.

The advantages of ISAs are that:

- You can use a different provider each year to take advantage of special offers, such as a higher rate of interest in a cash ISA, although such offers are usually available for only one year after which the rate of interest will drop to something less advantageous.
- You can cash in your ISA at any time if you need the money, so this is quite a good way to store 'rainy day' money. But remember that once you have withdrawn money from a particular ISA you will not be able to 'top up' your investment in that particular ISA afterwards.
- Any increase in value in a shares ISA will be tax free. This applies equally to individual shares held in an ISA as to shares held through a unit trust within an ISA.
- Some funds will permit you to set up direct debits so that you can invest money regularly. Even £20 per month will add up over the years.

Disadvantages:

- Investing in shares in an ISA 'wrapper' is just as risky as investing in shares; their value goes up and down in an ISA just as surely as if you bought the shares direct. You might need to sell them just at the time when their price plummets sharply in value.
- ISAs are really designed to be long-term investments. You will get the greatest benefit from them if you can leave them untouched for several years.

Before you make a decision to invest act as though you were advising a client and get as much information as you can by reading the financial pages of newspapers and reading specialist magazines. You may find that the library in your firm has lots of these available, but spending a few pounds on a specialist magazine for a couple of months and looking at the various comparison tables could help you to make the right decisions.

CREDIT CARDS AND STORE CARDS

Treat these with caution. Now that you have a regular income, probably above the national average, you will find credit cards and store cards relatively easy to obtain and they will come with a higher credit limit than you could obtain as a student. But remember that neglecting to pay back the outstanding balance as quickly as possible can increase your debt very quickly. Compound interest which is so useful in growing your pension contributions can also turn a small acorn debt into a substantial oak tree one very quickly. Just do the arithmetic on a 20% interest rate. You will never get that on your pension investment, but you could easily be charged it on a credit or store card.

Store cards are useful for:

- Taking advantage of special offers reserved for that store's card holders
- Taking advantage of additional 10% off days during annual sales
- Entries to free draws provided by some stores to their card holders – after all someone has to win the prizes
- Enabling you to pick up 'points' on purchases made in the store, which can be used to buy other items at that store

But remember that:

- You should always pay off store card balances first before the balance on any other sort of card, because they are likely to charge the highest rates of interest.
- It does take a long time to accumulate enough points to obtain anything significant in the way of vouchers, and most vouchers have a cut-off date which makes it difficult for you to accumulate the vouchers for anything other than a small purchase. Consider that these are really there to fund a small treat rather than to save for something big, and make the most of them by using them during sales periods if you can.
- Any special offers, additional 10% off promotions and vouchers are really designed to get you into the store to spend even more money, so that you need to exercise some self-discipline to resist their blandishments.

CREDIT CARDS

Credit cards are an easy way to pay for things. They obviate your having to carry cash around and are a necessity if you want to pay at once for an item which is more expensive than your cheque guarantee card will allow.

Like store cards some credit cards offer useful bonuses like money back on purchases or points which are totalled up and issued in the form of vouchers to be spent in particular stores. Remember that these are nice little perks amounting to 0.5–2% of the amount that you spend on your cards, but that you must also keep an eye on the interest rates that your credit cards charge on outstanding balances. The percentage perk does not look so enticing if it comes with a card that charges 23% on amounts outstanding and you regularly find that you cannot afford to pay off your debt at the end of the month. However, if you choose a card that earns you points or vouchers or repays a percentage of your spend AND you always pay off your card in full every month, you will effectively have made a little money by using your credit card. The only surefire way to ensure that your credit card debt is paid off in full every month is to set up a monthly direct debit at your bank so that you never run up credit card charges.

If the only way that you can pay for large purchases is to use a credit card and to pay the purchase price off over a period of months you should look for a credit card with a low interest charge or one with an interest-free period for balance transfers.

Office expenses

From time to time you'll need to dip into your own pocket temporarily to fund a work-related expense. This could be lunch for a client because your supervisor has left his wallet at home, or for a quick dash in a cab to file a document at court before it closes or for any number of other reasons. You can claim back legitimate work expenses only if you keep the receipt and if you know what it is for. Finding £50 of screwed up undated taxi receipts in a coat that you haven't worn for six months is not only annoying but it's bad for your finances. Keep a separate envelope or small plastic folder for receipts that need claiming back and write on the back of each exactly what they are related to, including the client or matter number before you put the receipts in the folder. You'll be surprised how much it all adds up to and having some sort of system will make claiming it back simple and straightforward rather than a headache and a hassle.

Don't take too long to claim back expenses – if you do you might find that the firm's Finance department refuse to reimburse you on the grounds that the client has long since been billed and the matter is now closed. You'll end up looking disorganised, being out of pocket and feeling disgruntled.

Yawn, yawn...

You can find all this advice and more ad nauseam in the personal finance pages of daily and weekly newspapers, and it is there because it is usually good advice that warrants repetition, as does the suggestion that if you need to borrow a large sum the first port of call should be your bank. Try out your persuasion skills successfully and you may be rewarded with a rate of interest which is much lower than any that you will be able to obtain on a credit card.

Whatever you do, keep an eye on the interest rates that you are being charged for borrowing and the interest rates that you are earning on your savings. And move your money around to get the best rates.

It is also worthwhile considering a card protection policy if you have credit cards. For an annual fee the card protection company will keep a note of all your credit card numbers so that if they are lost or stolen you need to make only one telephone call to cancel all the cards and arrange for new ones to be issued. This also effectively reduces the amount for which you are liable before you are able to report the loss or theft.

HOUSING

The beginning of your training contract may not be the ideal time to embark on buying your own home, but it is a good time to start thinking about it, especially if you are working in London or one of the other high demand/high cost housing areas. It can be tempting to splash out on the most spacious and best-situated flat that you can afford to rent with your friends, but it might be better to settle for a little less in order to be able to start saving for the deposit to get your foot on the first rung of the property ladder.

The chances are that you will not be able to do this alone, but think very carefully before you embark on buying a property with other people. It is much easier to walk away from a relationship that has gone sour if you are only renting. If you do decide to buy jointly – take proper legal advice! Make sure that you understand all the implications of holding property as joint tenants or as tenants in common, and also draft a separate document which sets out what will happen when one of you wants to sell and move on.

Chapter 17

PROTECTION AND SURVIVAL

SPEED READ SUMMARY

■ This chapter deals with protecting yourself, your firm and your clients.

■ Be careful what you say about your clients to people outside the firm and treat all client documents with the utmost care.

■ Don't be dishonest and don't tempt other people into dishonesty by leaving your own possessions and confidential client papers lying around.

■ Don't rely on legislation to protect you against harassment and bullying. You can save yourself pain and annoyance by learning how to read and avoid tricky situations.

CLIENT CONFIDENTIALITY

Make sure that you protect the firm's stock in trade – the confidential information given to it by its clients – by locking away your files when you are not using them. If you are not sure, put them away! Check your firm's data protection policy if it has one. In any event you and your firm are obliged under the Data Protection Act 1998 to make appropriate arrangements to keep personal data secure.

Not only do you need to lock away files, but you also need to take care with electronic data. Check your firm's data security policy which is likely to include the rule that all personal or sensitive data should be encrypted on laptops and portable drives/memory sticks. Take care whenever carrying around electronic data – the embarrassment to you and the firm could be huge if you lost it not to mention the trouble the firm could get into for breaching the Data Protection Act.

Don't gossip about your clients. Tax Inspectors and Customs Officers can tell you of countless instances when they have been able to prosecute tax dodgers because they have overheard two people discussing their financial affairs or those of their clients in public. Even if you are chatting on some tropical beach, remember that other professionals can afford to holiday there as well.

Never read confidential papers on public transport. You may be so engrossed in the heads of agreement for the sale of your client's business, that you may not notice that the innocuous-looking person sitting beside you is equally engrossed. And how would you know that he acts for the union representing the employees who will be affected by the proposed (and up until then, secret) disposal plans?

Remember that industrial espionage is a real possibility. Make sure that you shred any drafts referring to sensitive transactions and, particularly if you are engaged on something which is price sensitive, lock your screen when you are away from your desk. It's not just screen villains who have light keyboard fingers.

YOUR BELONGINGS

Law firms are just like any other workplace. Most of the time your belongings will be safe, but sometimes things will 'disappear'. It is therefore wise to take precautions. Don't leave keys and cash in your coat pockets. Either carry your handbag or wallet around with you when you move around the office or lock them away in a secure desk drawer. This may seem excessive but it is much less hassle than making a formal loss report, being interviewed by the police and having to replace missing items such as credit cards and house keys.

DON'T BE DISHONEST

Don't be tempted into even the smallest thefts and dishonesties. You may or may not be struck off for dangerous driving, drunk or disorderly conduct or having affairs with every partner in your firm, but you will not survive a criminal conviction for dishonesty. Solicitors deal with clients' money and the SRA deals very severely with anyone who is seen to fuel any misapprehension that solicitors are not a totally reliable and trustworthy profession.

If you have not yet obtained a training contract you will be unlikely to get one if you have any such conviction, even if it is 'only' fare-dodging on the London Underground.

After you have qualified, it is important to be even more vigilant because the opportunities for dishonesty may be that much greater. One wealthy partner took about £300 from his client account because he needed some ready cash. He fully intended to pay it back, but he forgot. His mistake was discovered in an audit trail and he was struck off. Negligence is not a defence to dishonesty. Even essentially honest people with the best of intentions can find themselves in serious trouble with the SRA if they are careless with their clients' money.

HARASSMENT AND BULLYING

It is a sad fact of legal life that many trainees and also many qualified solicitors find themselves victimised by bullies. What should you do if this happens to you? And how can you be certain that you are being harassed or bullied in the first place?

First of all try to understand why it happens. There is a difference between bullying and sexual harassment, although you could argue that sexual harassment is just another form of bullying. Before you categorise someone else's behaviour towards you, ask yourself whether it really is bullying or sexual harassment or whether it is simply rudeness or insensitivity.

Limitations of understanding

Bullying or harassment may also be the result of stress in a bully's own personal life. Perhaps the bully is in turn being bullied at home, perhaps is worried about an ailing parent, perhaps a spouse's insistence that the children are privately educated is becoming more and more difficult to fund, perhaps there are stress-related migraines or more serious health concerns. Although it can be useful to recognise this, you should never allow your understanding of someone else's personal circumstances to become a reason for continuing to be bullied. Even if the situation improves, the bully will have become used to being a bully and, worse still, you will become used to being a victim.

PRESSURE POINTS

The rewards and the pressures of working as a solicitor can be immense. It has taken you many years of education, some of it in very competitive circumstances, to get this far, and you will now have realised that if you want success in the legal world you will have to continue to work very hard. The legal press revel in league tables for types of work done, profits per equity partner, most lateral hires, even best flexible working practice. If your firm is sufficiently large the loss of an important client will be advertised in some legal journal within weeks, if not days. In order to survive the harsh reality of legal life, and even to get there in the first place, you need to be a particular type of person.

Many law firms teem not only with what are loosely called 'Type A' personalities, those who are driven by the thought of peer esteem, acclaim and money, but also with those who would like to be Type A personalities.

Such people achieve their success through hard work often to the exclusion of any real life outside the law village or at the expense of their family relationships. For some the office becomes their world, and many often begin to see themselves as barons with their own personal fiefdoms and their own personal serfs. There are many stories of businessmen who find themselves in prison for illegal activities involving often trivial sums compared to the amounts that they are really worth, who reply to the question, 'Why did you do it?' with the lame response, 'Because I could'.

Strange as it may seem, bullying can sometimes be a function of years of individuals requiring very high standards of themselves, whether in terms of quality of intellectual effort, cases won or even simply in terms of hours spent in the office. What they lose sight of as they castigate you for getting something wrong, or disdainfully toss a piece of your work back at you that has taken you hours to write, is the number of years of sheer hard grind that it has taken them to reach this powerful position. They are demanding perfection without giving you the time to achieve it. Such people are certainly not teachers or trainers and most likely they will never be satisfied with what you do just as they will never be satisfied with their own efforts.

ANALYSIS

Unfortunately behaviour which seems merely inappropriate to some people can be offensive to others. Comments which are considered as acceptable banter by one recipient may be regarded as sexist or racist insults by someone else. Some, but by no means all, of the comments which give offence are offensive because of:

■ the inequality of the positions of the parties concerned
■ the frequency of the comments
■ the timing of the comments

Being told that you 'look like a beached whale' when you are seven months pregnant may rankle a bit if the comment is made by a close friend or a work colleague with whom you have a long-standing collaborative relationship, but it takes on a totally different colour if it is made by someone who is in a senior position within the firm, and especially if it is made in front of other people. But is the comment grounds for a claim of bullying? Probably not. It's certainly an example of insensitivity and bad timing, and might make you wonder if you really want to return to the firm after maternity leave.

Being told that 'you Jocks are all the same, nobody can understand you' could be construed as a racist generalisation, but it could just be early morning banter between trainees provided that you can respond in kind that 'Liverpudlians can't speak English either.' It's an exchange of equals.

However, if you don't respond or if you indicate that you don't find this sort of thing funny and it is deliberately repeated, you would be right to be annoyed. But is it racial harassment?

On the other hand the repetition of unwelcome, personal comments, especially by a whole group of people, whether they have the same work status as you or not, could amount to harassment and your employer has a duty to provide you with a safe working environment where you can work to the best of your abilities.

SEXUAL HARASSMENT

A great many things could come under this heading: from pointedly looking at a particular part of someone's anatomy while speaking; implied or actual invitations to have sex, with or without the implication that your career might be affected by your compliance or refusal; right the way through to physically intrusive behaviour.

Some people certainly feel, either consciously or unconsciously, that their senior position gives them the right to 'try it on', whether or not you have indicated availability or encouragement. Others are simply not very good at understanding human relationships or reading the signs that say 'back off'. You should not accede to or tolerate the behaviour of either group, but there is much that you can do yourself to avoid uncomfortable situations.

Prevention

You may feel that the following comments in this section are overly prescriptive and that they do not reflect your own experience of work relationships in your office. Our comments are, however, based on the experiences of real lawyers who have found themselves in tricky situations which they afterwards felt might have been avoided if they had been a little more alert or had exercised a little more common sense.

Don't invite advances, either generally by wearing provocative clothing, flirting or by smiling coyly to someone more senior. If you think that this is unnecessarily restrictive, remember that you are in a workplace and not a singles club.

Two gins and a platonic, please

Don't go for drinks after work with a more senior colleague on your own unless you are sure that the relationship is entirely platonic. It can be difficult to decline such an invitation, especially if you have just completed a piece of work together, or it is the end of the day and you are on your way back to the office having been to a meeting at another firm.

Be honest with yourself. Are you perhaps secretly flattered that a senior colleague, maybe someone who is rich, powerful and clever, has specially invited you out? If you feel flattered and you suspect that an invitation is for more than an exchange of legal views, then you should definitely say no. Try to see the suggestion for what it is – a potentially very bad career move. But if you do find yourself going for a drink on an apparently platonic basis, don't give in to suggestions that you sit together in a cosy cubicle – stay in public view or perhaps stand at the bar. Make sure that you drink well within your capacity, and that you have an excuse ready so that you can leave at a reasonable hour.

Be careful when you and a more senior colleague are visiting a client in another part of the country or abroad and you have to book into a hotel. Don't fall for the 'let's consider this matter in my room, it's quieter there' or 'let's go for a drive and explore the area' routines and never, ever, in any circumstances permit your colleague to suggest that you have a drink in your hotel room after the bar has closed, because then you will be ceding control to someone who is more powerful than you, certainly in terms of your work but possibly physically as well. Also this can later be construed as you inviting that person into your room.

If you refuse to get yourself into this situation in the first place by pointing out that you really need a large amount of sleep if you are going to be able to do the best job you can for the client, it will do less damage to your career prospects than throwing someone out of your room at two am in the morning after an unsatisfactory tussle. The first indicates that you might, or might not, know what your colleague's intentions are, but nobody's pride is hurt. The second can end up with discomfort, frustration and annoyance on both sides.

Needless to say it is extremely important to monitor the amount that you drink while away from home – even the smallest drink can reduce your normal watchfulness or impair your judgement, especially if you haven't eaten much. Ignore the 'lightweight' jibes and the banter and stay well within your limit or better still stick to soft drinks. However enticing it might be to relax with a drink and the team while working on a big deal or when a case finishes, remember that they are your colleagues and not mates. Not all of your colleagues have your best interests at heart – you need to look after yourself and keep your career prospects safe; this is probably the last thing on your colleagues' minds but they should be the first thing on yours. In the cold light of day anything inappropriate that goes on will be remembered in the village forever, particularly if it involves you and a partner. A photograph taken on a mobile phone or an email could flash round the office in seconds or worse still round the world. Have you really studied all these years for your career to come to an ignominious end before it even gets going?

Try not to stay in the office alone with a colleague if you have any inkling that your colleague may be targeting you. This can be difficult, you may find yourself thinking up constant appointments, having a train to catch or suffering from headaches and insisting that you work better early in the morning than in the evening, but even though much of this may sound extremely pathetic and unfair to you, it's better than allowing a situation to get out of hand to the detriment of your career.

Take any comments made by your peer group about the predatory behaviour of other lawyers very seriously. Make sure that you do not offer unintentional encouragement and if possible try to find out more about the precise nature of the behaviour so that you can avoid putting yourself in awkward situations.

IF IT HAPPENS, WHAT ARE YOUR OPTIONS?

Whether or not you have allowed yourself to be in a situation where sexual harassment was predictable or whether the harassment was totally unexpected and uninvited, you should think very carefully before taking precipitate action. First, read the legislation, read the case law and then be realistic.

Does the behaviour that you are likely to complain of fall within the definition of behaviour that the law protects you against? Could you substantiate it with dates, times, places and details? Do you have any witnesses?

Unfair as it may seem, you are a trainee and it is likely that the person you are complaining of will be more senior, possibly worth a great deal to the firm in terms of client income and definitely worth more than you are. Law firms, in common with many other organisations, are very hierarchical and you are on the lowest rung of the hierarchy. Accusations of bullying or sexual harassment will therefore be very uncomfortable for the firm to investigate and support unless this sort of thing has happened before and/or you can corroborate your accusations, preferably with witnesses who are willing to support you.

Litigation

Is it worth taking your employer to court? Think about what you really want. If you are in a very senior position and can afford to take time out while you fight a court case and find another job, you may decide that it is worth it. However, if you are a trainee or are newly qualified with a great deal of debt, then it might, sadly, be better to get out than to fight, unless you really do have a cast iron case with many willing witnesses and some CCTV tapes. And even if you do, you should be aware that this sort of litigation takes its toll on your mental and physical health. It could literally make you ill.

SOME HARD QUESTIONS

If you decide that you do want to make a formal complaint, ask yourself what you want your firm to do.

Do you want the behaviour to stop? If the offending behaviour is 'merely' irritating, such as the 'beached whale' or 'Jockular' comments mentioned earlier, would its cessation be sufficient? If a more senior partner, possibly even the Senior or Managing Partner, is willing to have a word with the offender or offenders, this might be arranged, because no firm wants to find itself with a reputation for bullying or harassing its employees. If the behaviour does then stop, you will know that stern words have been spoken.

Do you want an apology? This is less likely but still possible if the Senior Partner and the firm consider that their colleague's behaviour is serious enough. You will then have to ask yourself how you deal with this apology. Telling everyone about it, although satisfying, will not be the best way to promote your future in the firm.

Do you want to move to another room and another supervisor if it is your supervisor who is bullying or harassing you? This might well be the best solution if the Managing or Senior Partner agrees to facilitate this, although you need to be aware that your new supervisor might either be very wary of you or alternatively might try to find out as many details as possible.

Whatever you decide to ask for, getting what you want is going to be uncomfortable, stressful, difficult and perhaps impossible. This is why it is better to avoid becoming a target.

Even harder questions

Do you need this job and the money that it pays badly enough either to put up with the inappropriate behaviour or to try to find alternative strategies to deal with it?

This is not to suggest that you should put up with inappropriate behaviour for money; that is prostituting your own standards for cash. However, it may dictate what you do to remove yourself from the situation or whether you are willing to embark on the process of obtaining a legal remedy. Certainly there are people who successfully sue their employers because they have been harassed or bullied, but read the press reports carefully and you will find that many are already wealthy individuals who can afford the substantial legal fees involved and whose career prospects may actually be enhanced by the publicity.

REMOVING YOURSELF FROM THE SITUATION

If you feel that the situation you are in is intolerable, get out! The longer you are bullied, the more difficult it will be to find another job, because the way that you have been treated will inevitably colour the way that you present yourself and influence the way that you answer that all important question, 'Dollar and Cash have an excellent Insurance Litigation department, so why would you want to leave them to come and do the same thing with us?'

No firm wants to take on someone who runs down their previous employer let alone someone who is, or may be, in dispute with another firm. Although in the abstract they may have sympathy with your tale of snide comments, belittling appraisals and touchy-feely supervisors, they

Sharpen your antennae

There are some situations which can develop into something more serious or can be adroitly nipped in the bud with few if any adverse consequences if you think all the options through carefully. One trainee was involved in a major deal with a long-standing client of her firm. After a couple of weeks of very long meetings involving her, the client and her supervising partner, she came in to work one morning to find that a messenger had delivered a magnum of expensive vintage champagne from the client. With a handwritten message that said 'I think we should discuss this further... '

As he had taken to staring at her somewhat appraisingly over the past couple of days, she felt that the invitation in the message was fairly clear. What should she do? If she accepted the champagne, the client might be encouraged to take a bolder step. If she returned it, he might be so offended by the rebuff that he might take his future business elsewhere. If she said that she did not want to work on this particular matter any more, she would lose valuable experience.

She thought quickly, put the bottle on her supervising partner's desk without the note, and said cheerfully when he came in, 'This has just been delivered from Mr Smoothy.' When the partner thanked Mr Smoothy a few days later for the 'handsome magnum of champagne which my family enjoyed very much,' there were no repercussions.

Another young lawyer's client got rather too close to her to tell her that she had 'such a tiny waist'. She smiled and said 'Yes, and my husband thinks so too.'

Yes, you do need a quick wit, but it could save you a lot of time and legal fees.

will be concerned that the situation is not as one-sided as you have depicted it. And remember that just as you have friends in other firms, it is just possible that the partners who are interviewing you may have an amicable (or marital) relationship with the colleagues that you are complaining about and want to escape from.

If you do leave you need to have a good story. Don't bad-mouth the firm that you are leaving, because the new one will be looking for team players. Firms want to believe that the person they are interviewing wants to join them because of their excellent reputation, glowing future and maybe even high salaries. They certainly do not want to believe that any village will suffice because the old one has become too hot for you to handle.

GOING TO HR

Going to HR to complain or even to ask for advice about the inappropriate behaviour of one of your more senior colleagues may seem like the right thing to do, but this can sometimes backfire. One senior assistant relatively new to a firm consulted HR as to how she should deal with the repeated sexual invitations of her departmental head. The immediate comment was that 'perhaps you don't fit into this firm', followed the next day by a formal complaint from the partner concerned about the quality of her work and an attempt to dismiss her. After advice from the employment department of another firm and several months of preparation for litigation she settled with the firm for a substantial sum.

This was not however what she had wanted in the first place. All she had wanted was some informal advice, but she soon found that HR felt obliged to treat it as a formal complaint which escalated into a bruising experience. HR can never promise you absolute confidentiality so don't think that they can. Once you have unburdened yourself by telling a member of HR they may feel they are obliged to pass on what you discussed and they might not even tell you that they have done so.

A moment's reflection should make you realise that it would almost be negligence on the part of any HR professional, whether in a law firm or in any other organisation, not to consult senior management about instances of harassment or bullying.

Chapter 18

APPRAISAL INTERVIEWS

SPEED READ SUMMARY

■ Appraisal interviews usually result in a written report that will go on your personal file. Preparing for them in advance will help you direct your supervisor to write down the most positive comments.

■ Before the interview list all that you have learned and what you have achieved since your last appraisal.

■ Think about how you can:

  – explain your shortcomings and how you propose to deal with them

  – help your supervisor and the firm

■ If you want to go on external courses, be able to explain how they would help not only you but the work of the firm. Have information ready and be willing to organise them.

■ Agree your appraisal summary with your supervisor.

■ And afterwards – act on what was agreed in the interview.

BEING APPRAISED

During the course of your training contract and at the end of it, you will be expected to take part in appraisal interviews. This is a means of assessing your performance. Although there is a difference between training contract interviews and internal appraisal interviews, there is also a common thread. Many of the comments made in Chapter 2 will also be relevant here, except that you now know the people interviewing you. Appraisal interviews are therefore likely to have the appearance of informality, but you should not assume that they are really cosy fireside chats between work colleagues.

PREPARING YOUR EVIDENCE

Before you go into an appraisal make a list of the work that you have done since the last one, and think about the good things that clients or other lawyers have said to you or about you.

It's a good idea to get a folder and to keep a copy of every good result or letter of thanks or record of achievement. Don't think of it as a 'boasting book' but rather as something to help you to remember the good stuff. A quick read through before your internal appraisal or next time you go for an external interview should help you to feel positive about yourself. Be your own Number One Fan! In addition, if you know you have fans (a partner at home, a friend or a colleague), ask them what they think your achievements are. Often they will say something that you haven't thought of.

Good appraisal systems will allow for exchange of pre-appraisal preparation documents so that what you have to say to your appraiser and vice versa should not come as a surprise. But not all firms will have effective appraisal processes, so make sure that you prepare and perhaps let your appraiser see what you have written before you meet even if your appraiser doesn't do likewise.

PRESENTING YOUR CASE

It's important that your supervisors know what you have learned, what you have achieved and how much you have been appreciated by others. This is not bragging. It's up to you to ensure that your supervisors know about your progress since the last appraisal, not least because they have been busy and probably will not have noticed half of what you have been achieving. It could come up quite conversationally:

- 'I thought that it was going to be difficult to deal with the Chief Executive of a major public company like Imperial Widgets, but then I

realised that when you do a good job for him he will treat you very fairly.'
- 'It was good fun working on that licence application, and it gave me a real buzz when it was over and the client sent me round a bottle of champagne.'
- 'The first time that I did a distributor fund application it seemed very complicated, but then I realised that it's all about taking care and paying attention. It seems to me that many of these will be roughly the same. Would it be a good idea for me to set up a pro forma application to help the next trainee who comes along?'

However, don't launch into a detailed blow-by-blow and legislative-reference-by-legislative-reference account of how you solved a particularly tricky problem unless you are asked to do so. This is not the appropriate forum for a 15-minute analysis of the VAT complications of supplies made between a Head Contractor and the Sub-contractor in a mixed development. All your supervisor needs is the quiet reminder that your burning of the midnight oil saved the client £200,000 in VAT and that the client was very happy to pay his bill promptly.

If possible, try to compliment your firm in some way:
- 'I was very glad that you gave me the opportunity to take the notes of the meeting at SharkBank, because when they phoned me up and you weren't there I was able to deal with their query.'

Talk it up!

Most things that you do can be made to sound better than they may seem to you. And most things can be made to sound worse. It has been said that men come to their annual reviews with coloured charts and a list of things they have achieved, but that women come with five things they should have done better. Whether or not you think that this gender-directed statement is true, think about it and whether it could apply to you.

One successful entrepreneur when giving a broad-brush estimate of something was adept at doubling the good numbers and halving the bad ones. Strangely enough this often had the result of influencing others to produce exactly the results that he wanted.

The worst thing that you can do at an appraisal interview is to belittle your achievements and concentrate on what you can't do. Self-deprecation is not a winning attribute in a law firm – endearing (perhaps) as it might be for a moment, you could just as easily leave others with the impression that you are 'too wet' or 'too weak' for the harsh realities of legal practice.

HOW TO DEAL WITH YOUR FAILINGS

Do take some time to think about your shortcomings before you go in. But also consider what positive action you can take to deal with them. Then if your supervisor does mention any of your failings you will be ready with a positive strategy. And phrase it properly. If your supervisor comments that your grasp of the latest Children Act is a little tenuous, then be ready to say something along the lines of 'Yes, I noticed that the library had a new commentary and I am spending some time reading that.' Show that you are aware of any deficiencies and that you have already worked out how to tackle them.

But don't bring them up first. If your supervisor has not noticed them, why should you give him something negative to put on your appraisal form? Don't bring the word 'confidence' into the conversation in a negative way, such as 'I don't feel very confident about that yet' or 'I'm sure that I'll feel more confident about doing that on my own very soon.' Your supervisor will not notice the qualifiers 'yet' or 'very soon' but will certainly remember that you said that you were 'not confident' about something. Your firm does not want to be employing people who indicate that they are diffident about what they are doing.

MAKING SUGGESTIONS

When you join a firm or department you will inevitably notice that things are done in a certain way. With the eyes of a newcomer you might well think that they could be done differently. Don't dismiss this as an idle thought and that everyone else knows better. Tactfully raise your suggestion. It may be a brilliant idea that no one else has thought of because they are so used to doing things in a certain way. Being brand new can sometimes be a big advantage.

If you have actively helped to improve the efficiency of your department by creating precedent letters or practice notes or by organising information in a more easily accessible way, then find a way to drop that into the interview conversation if your supervisor does not do so.

Taking the initiative in small things which improve the comprehensibility of complex arrangements will demonstrate an organised mind. One trainee became so frustrated with having to find papers over several files relating to the distribution of probate property that he took the time to produce a 'black book' which had indexed photocopies of the relevant documents and plans together with a short commentary. This was the sort of work that no one would have given to a qualified solicitor because it was strictly speaking work that was difficult to charge for, but it made it very much easier for the partner concerned to hand on the matter to subsequent trainees; and it was always handed on with a statement of praise for the trainee who had produced it in the first place.

If you are simply making your supervisor's life more congenial because you are relatively easy to get on with, are tidy but not noisy, there will probably be a note in your file indicating that you are 'a pleasant person to share a room with'. Slight as it may seem, don't underestimate the praise in that comment, because no one wants to share with a bumptious, unhelpful colleague.

HOW CAN YOU IMPROVE YOUR SUPERVISOR'S LIFE?

The one thing that supervisors are always short of is time. If you can create more of that scarce commodity by being organised yourself and by anticipating that certain books or papers will be required and making sure that they are there, you will create a very good impression. Make sure that the files that you share are neat, that you know their contents and that you can also quickly access the contact details of clients and the lawyers on the other side. Yes, in theory this is a secretarial job, but it will not be the secretary who will be there at eight pm – it will be you.

Although filing should not be an end in itself, good filing, whether by you or your secretary, can make your life a whole lot easier and your ability to locate information quickly, even if you do not understand its full implications, will impress.

One good habit that you should adopt from day one is to keep your daily notes in a Daybook and not on loose pieces of paper. If you are involved in only one or two large matters at a time, then you could keep one Daybook per matter. If on the other hand you are working for several people or you are asked to deal with several smaller matters at a time, you could keep just one Daybook.

Whatever you do, make sure that you:
- Name, number and date the cover of each one
- Enter the date at the beginning of each day
- Do not destroy them unless you are requested to do so, perhaps where there is a proposed M&A (Merger and Acquisition) bid which has failed
- Do not jettison them when you move on to your next seat, and certainly

don't toss them casually into a waste-paper bin. (If you do get rid of them later – shred them. Remember client confidentiality.) You are quite likely to be quizzed on an issue on an ongoing matter that you dealt with two years previously. Being able to access your notes and therefore the relevant information quickly can save you a lot of time.

You can use them to help you to prepare good handover notes for the incoming trainee, before suggesting that you meet up for an hour over tea to talk through outstanding issues. As well as being a sensible bonding exercise, it will refresh your memory about what you have been doing over the last six months.

THE YEAR AHEAD

Your supervisor will probably ask you in your interview what you hope to achieve in the next six months or a year. Your immediate response might be to say 'earn more money for the firm'. That is taken for granted. The more serious question is, 'How are you going to do it?'

Making a broad general statement of intent when you have not really thought through its implications lays you open to reeling off a long list of activities in which you might engage in order to boost your and the firm's profitability. And make no mistake, the casual suggestion that you throw out to fill up the conversational space because you have come to the end of your list of suggestions will be noted and remembered at the next appraisal, and you will be asked how successful you have been in achieving it.

So give some thought to this before the interview, and think of something better than Boxer's promise in *Animal Farm* that 'I must work harder.' Make sure that it is something that you can actually deliver. Don't think that because you are moving to another department after six months that what you say will be forgotten. It will not, it will form part of the basis for your next interview with your next supervisor. 'I see that you said that you would have written a client note on Home Information Packs by the end of your seat in Residential Property. Did you succeed in doing that? You didn't? Why was that?'

WHAT CAN YOUR FIRM DO FOR YOU?

Appraisal interviews are meant to be a two-way process. Your firm should be interested in your becoming a good lawyer and this is the time to ask for what you want in terms of external course provision or professional journals or books. The willingness or otherwise of the firm to help you and your professional development will give you an idea of:

- What the partners think of your future prospects in the firm.
- How forward-looking they are about the future of the firm or their department, and how much they are willing to develop it. Are they simply going through the motions of ensuring that everyone can tick the box on the PQE form, or do they really care about what their trainees and young solicitors are learning?
- How profitable the firm is. If the firm is not making sensible money, there will certainly be no money for external training.

However, there may be perfectly good reasons why the firm may not want to send you on a particular course. Perhaps they have already arranged for someone else to attend it who will later give a summarised version to the rest of the department, or they may simply have found that courses given by that particular provider are not good value for money.

APPRAISAL SKILLS

You will have realised by now that the effective conduct of interviews of any sort is a high-level skill that not everyone possesses and appraisal interviews are no exception. Some supervisors feel that they are simply a waste of valuable work time and others, with the best will in the world, find the whole process uncomfortable.

Some firms send supervisors on courses to help them, some do not. Some supervisors take the appraisal process very seriously and see it as an opportunity to sum up the past few months and to learn themselves about how they could in the future treat their trainees better. And some do not.

TURNING NEGATIVE INTO POSITIVE

Here again, it's up to you to be proactive and to make sure that at the end of the interview you have something positive to take away. And to make sure that even the apparently negative things are framed positively.

- Your departmental presentation on the Mental Capacity Act which was inadequate, because you had not realised that you were meant to be speaking for 20 minutes rather than five, could result in the positive comment on your file that 'X now understands the importance of proper preparation.' The idea is to turn the failure into an apparently positive learning experience.
- Your tendency to skip through work without paying proper attention to

detail could be criticised or could, with a little bit of guidance from you, go down as 'X works very fast, and could afford to take a little more time over drafting without jeopardising agreed billing targets.'

At the end of each section of the appraisal:
- Summarise any suggestions as to how you could improve your work in a way that is comfortable for you. 'So you would like me to… '
- Negotiate realistic deadlines. 'Next week or next month or by the time that I leave the department.'

If you don't think that deadlines are doable, say so. You don't want your supervisor asking the next trainee to take over something, because X didn't manage to finish it' when the deadline was unrealistic in the first place. The new trainee will get the kudos and you will have the unwelcome mantle of being seen as not being a completer/finisher.

If you had pointed out in the first place that it would be unlikely that you could get it done by the time that you left the department but that you would do half of it and would ensure that the next trainee would be fully apprised of what was required to finish it, then you will have covered yourself. And you might actually get it finished.

UNDER-PROMISE BUT OVER-DELIVER
If you want to impress, always keep this Golden Rule in mind.

Be honest if it is not going to be possible to fulfil some sort of developmental target unless you drop something else. Then negotiate what is going to be dropped. The worst thing that you can do is to leave an appraisal with a list of things that you have promised to do when you know that you cannot do all of them. When the next appraisal is due someone will have a piece of paper in front of them where they will tick off eight out of the ten things that you said you would do, and then focus on the two on which you did not deliver. Remember once again that 80% is not good enough.

If you want external training, ask for it and be positive and helpful about it. Speak to the PSL/Training department/HR and go along armed with some suggestions. Show that you have the initiative to take responsibility for your own professional development.

Involve your supervisor and the assessing partner in the selection of the training course. Don't simply 'ask' to go on 'a training course', make sure that you have done some research first, including on course content and cost and then ask for their advice on how to proceed. 'I've seen this course that would... ' or 'What do you think would be the best course for me to... ' 'Who is the best authority on... ' If you can avoid it, try not to present them with the thought that they need to think carefully about whether you should go on a course, any course, in the first place.

THE APPRAISAL FORM

The tangible evidence of your appraisal is a form which should be signed as a true record by both you and your supervisor. If you do not agree with what is written, then you can in theory refuse to sign it, but it will still go on your file as a manager's appraisal. However, you can also ask the HR department for the opportunity to put a short note on your file indicating that you do not agree with the other person's appraisal. You will only want to do this if the comments are denigratory or you are stated to have agreed to do things which are impossible or unrealistic. The better bet is to try to influence what is written on the form even before your supervisor's pen is poised over the paper, because most supervisors who are pressed for time will be writing notes for the appraisal form, if not actually filling in the form itself, while you are talking.

Rather than leave any discussion about your performance to the official appraisal sessions, be proactive and engineer frequent informal two-way chats. You may not always like what you hear, but you will have more chances to improve your performance and to explain what you have found less easy (don't say 'difficult') without it being recorded on an official form. This will also give you the opportunity to remind your supervisor at the formal appraisal session just how much you have improved.

Some hard-pressed – or lazy – supervisors will ask you to fill in the appraisal form that they are supposed to complete. Now there's a challenge. It can be difficult to steer the right course between being totally immodest and arrogant and totally self-critical and sycophantic.

Proactive reports

An appraisal should be a dialogue about your past and future achievements, not a one-sided critique of your past failings, and the completed appraisal form should be a fair record of that dialogue.

In an ideal world the words that go down on your appraisal form should not be:

- 'X needs help with Y'
- 'X is not good at drafting, and is verbose'
- 'X does not have a good telephone manner'
- 'X has a tenuous grasp of... '

But

- 'Within the next three months X will attend a course on... '
- 'X will get more practice with drafting over the next six weeks; X will consult HR to find a suitable drafting course. Have recommended that X reads Gowers' *Complete Plain Words*.'
- 'Y will arrange for X to speak to the Head Telephonist within the next week.'

In other words, at the end of your meeting you will have an individual plan with specific goals and timescales that will support your development as a lawyer. As not all supervisors see this as the goal of an appraisal meeting be prepared to guide them gently in this direction.

If you have managed this part of the appraisal process properly, the question at your next appraisal should not be, 'Is your drafting any better?' but 'How did the course on drafting go? What did you think of it? What did you learn from it?'

PREPARING FOR YOUR NEXT APPRAISAL

Don't scurry out of the room as soon as you possibly can. Make sure that you have noted the most important action points – yes, you too should take notes. Smile and thank your supervisor for his time even if he is someone that you share a room with. After all he may have had much more pressing things to do and may feel just as uncomfortable with the whole process as you do.

Don't simply close the door, heave a sigh of relief that it was not too bad, that they have not asked you to leave, return to your office and carry on as normal because, after all, you have survived.

Make a note of what you said that you would do and what aspects of your work came up that need improvement. This is the point at which you start preparing for your next appraisal. It is all too easy to go back to your desk and get immediately wrapped up in client work. Before you know it your next appraisal will be due and the course that you specifically requested has not even been booked or you have not arranged to speak to the individual whom your supervisor thought might help you. Display the agreed actions for the next period on a pin board or inside the front cover of your Daybook as a reminder of what you need to do – and make sure that you act on the reminders!

THEN TAKE THE FIRST STEPS

- If courses need to be organised, follow the firm's procedure for booking yourself a place
- If books need to be read, at least find out where they are and, even better, get them onto your desk
- If you need to speak to someone, make an appointment
- Set reminders in your diary so that you can check how your improvement plans are progressing

APPRAISE YOUR APPRAISER

Having done all this, sit back and ask yourself honestly how your supervisor felt about conducting the appraisal. If he came prepared with notes or had at least clearly thought about it, entered into a reasonable dialogue with you and listened to what you said, made notes and made helpful suggestions and praised you where possible, this is as it should be.

If on the other hand he came in, said something along the lines of 'Let's get this rigmarole over with as quickly as we can,' made no notes, concentrated on your shortcomings or offered no constructive comments on how you might develop over the next few months, then you should seriously consider what you are doing working for this person. You may not have any control over this as a trainee, but you should think seriously about whether you would want to work for him as a newly qualified solicitor if you are offered a job in his department, however fascinating you find the work.

Chapter 19

SECONDMENTS AND OVERSEAS SEATS

SPEED READ SUMMARY

■ Many firms offer trainees the opportunity to do a seat or part of a seat away from the home office.

■ Seconding trainees to clients can have a three-way benefit. The firm builds a closer relationship with the client, the client gets ongoing assistance without engaging another employee and the trainee gets valuable commercial experience.

■ It is vital to prepare for secondment by finding out as much as possible about the client.

■ You will be an interface between the client and your firm. No one expects you to know everything, especially at first, but you need to make it as easy as possible for the client to get sound legal advice as quickly as possible.

■ Working in an overseas office can be similar to secondment, but at a distance. Although you will need to be much more alert to cultural differences, on the positive side you will be working in a legal environment and you may have the opportunity to save some money for your return.

PRACTICAL LEARNING

It's easy to assume that the only way that you can learn is 'at the feet of the master' in the office. However, many firms offer trainees the opportunity to do a seat or part of a seat away from the home office. Firms with overseas offices or which have 'swap' arrangements with law firms abroad usually provide at least some of their trainees with the opportunity of overseas experience. The other way that trainees may acquire out-of-office experience is through secondment to one of the firm's clients.

SECONDMENTS

Some firms 'loan' trainees or junior assistants on a regular basis to particular clients with whom they have a long-standing relationship and others supply trainees on an ad hoc basis to satisfy a need that the client has at that particular time.

The work that you are likely to get will be confined to a particular industry or endeavour and is probably going to be more commercial and practical than the work that you would get in the office in that particular area. In a law firm Property department you might have to consider a wide variety of property issues from the liability for fence repair between properties to complex lease provisions in a major development. If you are seconded to a property developer you will be very unlikely to deal with the first sort of problem and be much more likely to deal with the second.

Some quasi-governmental organisations also take secondees on a fairly regular basis. Your firm may or may not already be the recipient of work from the organisation, but its reason for seconding you may not lie in the

---

Key skills

On a secondment you will have more apparent responsibility more quickly because there will not be a supervisor sitting in the same room.

There are two key skills that you will have to learn in this situation:

■ The first is being able to assess what you can safely tackle yourself and what will require input from more senior lawyers at your own firm.

■ The second is how you impart information to the company to which you are seconded. They will not be impressed if every time you are asked a question you say, 'I don't know'. Equally they will not be impressed if you take a stab at an answer, then forget what you have said about it, they act on your erroneous advice and then lose an investment opportunity or several thousand pounds as a result.

hope of immediate work. It may simply be that the firm wants to broaden your experience, or that they want to find out a bit more about the workings of the particular organisation or simply that there is a drought of work in your particular specialism but they do not want to lose trainees or newly qualified lawyers whom they see as being part of their future plans.

Benefits to you

You will be working directly with a client, learning about that client's business without the interface of your supervisor, although you will still have the safety net beneath you of being able to consult your colleagues back at base if you feel out of your depth.

You will learn from the client's perspective what clients expect of lawyers, what irritates them (broken promises and sloppy work) and what they value (the opposite). Perhaps most important of all you will learn about building relationships with clients, so that you are both comfortable working together.

You will obtain greater exposure to the client's senior management. Remember that you will not be a trainee or a junior lawyer forever. Because you may well be the only lawyer or one of very few at the client company, you may be accorded a lot more respect and taken a lot more seriously than if you were back at your own office. If you impress, you will be remembered and may well be the one contacted by that client in future when legal advice is required. Some secondees have subsequently been delighted to accept permanent in-house roles with the client once they have qualified.

Preparation

Think of a secondment as being a mark in your favour as your own firm wants the client to whom you are seconded to be impressed with you. It does not want you to disappoint them to the extent that they never want your firm's services again. So, before you go, take some time to:

- Find out as much as you can about the client. Do an internet search, do a Companies House search and particularly trawl the press for information about the client's key players. If on your first day you are called in to see Mr X, it could just help to know if Mr X is the Finance Director or a member of the Accounts Staff. Are there any highly publicised deals in which the client has been involved?
- Find out if the client is the subject of any disputes with their employees. Knowing this in advance might prevent you making a social gaffe in an

unhappy department. How well is the client doing? The general atmosphere in an office will be affected by how well or badly the client is doing at the time. If your temporary colleagues are concerned about their jobs, they may well be less friendly towards you than otherwise. If you are prepared in advance for this possibility, you might be able to take being bawled out for some minor infraction less personally.

- Find out something about the client's commercial competition. Again you should at least know the names of the key competitors in their field.
- Speak to any trainees or lawyers who have previously been seconded to that organisation. Find out as much as you can about the work and about the 'power lines' at the client – this can help when you are prioritising your work.
- Find out if any of your client's personnel were formerly lawyers at your firm, why they left and most importantly what is the current relationship between them and your firm. Your firm may have found them sadly lacking in the technical skills department and made them painfully aware of it, but the client to whom they were seconded may have recognised the superb organisational skills which they could provide. You may therefore find yourself in the difficult position of being asked for unsavoury gossip and criticism of what was their former firm, but what is now yours. Resist this invitation. You will most likely be going back to your firm, where by devious means it may have reached the head of your department that you think that she is a 'beastly workaholic who neglects her children', or that the Senior Partner is 'interested only in working his staff to death so that he can buy more pictures for his private collection and schmooze members of the Royal Family'.
- Arm yourself with information about the latest cases and the latest legislation which might affect your client's business. You do not need to know this in detail – yet – but you should at least be able to understand why it is important.

Fielding legal questions

Most likely you will be dealing with documentation, which gives you a little more time to consider things, but do make sure that you understand all the legislative references in the documentation, so that you are not caught out when negotiating on behalf of the client.

But sometimes, you will be asked a direct, and important, question.

If at all possible, take the time to think about it. Your client will not want an academic research paper, but a short practical answer, along the lines of 'yes, you can do that' or 'you would be unwise to do that'. Although you are only a trainee your client may well regard you as having more knowledge than you possess and ask you the really tricky question, 'What is the likelihood of my being able to do... ?'

Clients are particularly interested in the likelihood of being caught out by regulatory authorities or by HM Revenue and Customs. This is not surprising. When you are dealing with contractual matters between two consenting parties there is always the possibility of renegotiation or settlement of liabilities. Where some sort of public authority is involved settlement may be possible, but so also may be fines or criminal prosecution.

Don't be tempted to answer a question which asks something apparently vague such as, 'What are the chances that the Revenue will look behind this contract?' A guess won't do. You simply do not have the experience to be able to assess how a public body is likely to jump on any particular issue. It takes years of experience to be able even to be aware of all the factors that would need to be considered to come up with any reasonable appraisal of the way the Revenue or any other regulatory authority will view a situation.

Don't try to fudge it by saying something innocuous like '50/50'. There may just have been a decision in a case, which indicates either that your client would be a fool to attempt to build on a particular site or there is a strong industry rumour that the VAT on substantial refurbishment is likely to be reduced in the forthcoming Budget. This is definitely a time when you need to refer to higher authority. It's best to advise simply that. 'I'd like to consult one or two of my colleagues before I come up with a definitive answer.'

Get the facts, consult, advise and note

Whatever you are asked to do, try not to give a glib, off-the-cuff answer. It's OK to say that you'd like to check a point or that the question is really interesting and complex and that you would not like to waste your interlocutor's time with idle speculation. Ascertain the facts and then get on the phone to someone who can help you...

But before you do that, think through the issue as far as you can, do a bit of research, so that you can give the impression to the person you consult back at your firm that you have thought about the problem and simply want confirmation that your analysis is correct. And make a contemporaneous note of what is said and agreed between you. If a similar question arises again, the client will expect you to be able to answer it and your supervisor will not want to be bothered a second time with the same question.

Secondment downsides

Any disadvantages to being seconded flow from the simple fact that for a time you will be living in a different village in a different part of the commercial world.

The rules will be different. The working hours will be different. You may feel cut off or isolated from your law firm village and the support of your peers. You may also find you have a long, tedious commute because it simply isn't practical to move home for the duration of the secondment. The rewards for the people you work with will be different from those in your home village – in a regulatory authority they will be less, and in a bank they could be astronomically more. The unspoken assumptions around the social aspects of office life will be different. If you are a woman, you may well find that the way that you are treated is different. The office tensions will be around different things.

This could be upsetting, but it could also be enormously mind-broadening and productive as you will be exposed to how other people work. At the end of your secondment you may well return to your firm with an enormous sigh of relief or, on the other hand, submit your resignation because you have found what you truly want to do. The thing to remember is that even hard and difficult experiences are good if you know how to value them.

Don't drift away from your village

In some cases you will have little choice about keeping in touch with your firm while you are on secondment. There may be a negotiated requirement that you attend monthly departmental meetings and seminars or you may be working with members of your firm on matters for the client to whom you are seconded. In other cases there may be little or no expectation that you will have contact with your firm unless you need some help.

While it can be very tempting to immerse yourself in the other village experience to the exclusion of your own firm, try to take a wider view. Six or even three months is a long time to be out of your usual village routine. People will have left, new people will have arrived, promotions will have happened, new alliances will have been forged and old ties fractured. Your firm will have lost clients and gained clients. The world will have moved on.

On a professional level, legislation, case law and custom and practice will have moved on as well. You may have spent a very valuable six months with a property developer involved in negotiating with landowners, architects and local authorities concerning an out-of-town shopping centre or may have worked happily (and with shorter hours) in the Legacy department of a charity that your firm supports, but the relevance to your firm will most likely not be immediate. It is important that you have not lost touch with the work that they want you to do when you return from 'your sabbatical' – some of your colleagues will see it like that. So, try if at all possible to keep up-to-date, even in the sketchiest of ways. To misquote Alexander Pope, in this case 'a little knowledge is a valuable thing', provided that you use it as a pointer to the additional stuff that you need to know and not as a total resource.

Keep in touch with your friends at the firm. Not only can you glean a lot of information over a quick lunch or drink after work, or after a football or squash match, but it will be easier for them to slot you back into their routine when you return. In other words don't underestimate the effects of dislocation.

OVERSEAS SEATS

Many of the same comments could be applied to doing a seat in one of your firm's overseas offices, except that everything is enhanced or exacerbated.

- You get to see how other offices in the same global firm function
- You get the experience not just of another village but of a village in another culture altogether
- You can form close relationships with young lawyers from other global firms which can prove more than useful in the future
- You can hone your language skills, or acquire some. Although English is rapidly becoming the international commercial language, it will be impossible to avoid the use of a second or third language in your everyday life outside the office.

Financial improvement

Sometimes doing an overseas seat can radically improve your financial position. You will most probably be provided with accommodation or at least a housing allowance in addition to an overseas allowance. If you are able to let your own home while you are away, you might be able to accumulate some cash as well as having some excellent experience in another culture. However, don't go abroad purely with a financial motive.

You may not be able to or may not be in a position to let your UK accommodation (your parents may not take kindly to finding a complete stranger in the room that you keep at their home), and the temptations of expatriate life may be too strong.

Doing a seat overseas often has one big disadvantage – coming back. Imagine how it feels landing at Heathrow in freezing fog in January having left behind an enhanced income in a warm climate and a buzzing social life. That could be the reality – so just prepare for it. Coming back can be a big upheaval personally, financially and socially; don't expect it to be easy.

Do the seat if other considerations are persuasive, but as with other life decisions don't let the financial dog wag the tail of the rest of your life.

Being there

Foreign offices are subject to exactly the same tensions as the office back home. And then some. This is particularly true if the office is a small one, or if the foreign practice is a joint one staffed by nationals from the host culture. This is when you discover that those little nuances of facial expression, tone of voice and use of simple everyday words have different meanings in other parts of the world, and that in some cultures what is apparently courtesy is actually a way of avoiding coming to a conclusion.

There may also be added tensions between the UK office and the foreign office because the foreign office partners feel that their opinions and concerns are regarded as of small importance by the 'Head Office'. You, as a recent arrival from the mother ship, may find that you are being pumped for the latest gossip and current positioning of partners back home. This is where you need to become an instant diplomat, giving just enough information to keep your new supervisors onside but remembering that what you say in Hong Kong could find its way back to London or Manchester. In other words, all the skills that you needed in your home village could be even more necessary here.

Fortunately there will often be trainees or newly qualified lawyers in your firm whom you can pump for information. Don't confine this information search to what's hot in local nightlife or where is the best place to get a good deal on suits or sushi. It will save you a lot of learning time and potential embarrassment if you go armed with information about the office power lines, the expected dress code and attitudes to client entertaining and office expenses. More importantly some understanding of any local law that you will be dealing with and its basis will be very helpful, as will any basic familiarity with local languages.

A creditable performance during the seat may lead at some point in the future to the offer of a two-year associate position. As you will be working

---

The female perspective

If you are a woman, it is crucial to find out what the cultural expectations are for your gender. You might not like what you hear, but remember that your function in the six months or so that you are there is not to change their attitude to women but to learn as much as you can and to work out how and whether you could operate in that environment. Your foreign office experience may just give you the edge when clients from that country visit your home office in the UK.

One very tall female lawyer found that she earned the respect of Japanese clients and lawyers with whom she had to deal simply by sitting down as soon as possible in any meeting so as not to look down on them.

---

overseas you may count as 'non-resident' for UK tax purposes and thus will not have to pay UK tax on your overseas earnings. You will be liable for tax in the country in which you are working but in some countries this may be at a lower rate, thus giving you the opportunity to save substantial amounts of money. But, as usual, check the current tax position before you factor any money-making potential into your decision.

Chapter 20

SHOULD I STAY OR SHOULD I GO?

SPEED READ SUMMARY

■ Before qualification you should consider whether you wish to remain with your present firm, or indeed whether there is likely to be an appropriate position available for you. Make an informed decision about your next move.

■ Appraise your current firm by considering the type of work they offer, the type of clients they have and how they are regarded externally.

■ Even if the firm is well thought of, look carefully at the structure of any department you would consider working in and ask yourself what would be your promotion prospects and whether you would be likely to flourish there.

■ Assess yourself carefully and ask yourself whether the work on offer would really suit your skills and inclinations.

■ If you do decide to leave your current firm remember that the Exit Interview can be another Elephant Trap.

POST-QUALIFICATION CHOICES

Before you begin reading this chapter, think 'I am valuable' not 'Aren't I lucky that this firm put up with me for the duration of my training contract?'

The tone of this chapter is intentionally sceptical. Having completed your training contract you will have come to the end of a long process of formal education which has given you a highly sought-after qualification and which can open doors to many careers other than a legal one. You owe it to yourself to take the time to assess yourself, your training experience and your firm before you accept the first legal opening that is offered to you.

Even before the end of your training contract you should be thinking about what comes next. Just in case, keep your CV up-to-date in the same way that you record your achievements as you go along for your appraisal. You should keep it updated with brief descriptions of additional experiences, new skills you have acquired, courses you have attended, articles you have written and seminars you have delivered. Updating your CV as you go along is sensible preparation for the future, as you never know when you might meet someone who invites you to 'send us your CV'. It's also a manifestation of your belief in yourself and proves that you are taking responsibility for your most valuable asset – you.

It may already be apparent that you need to look for a job elsewhere.

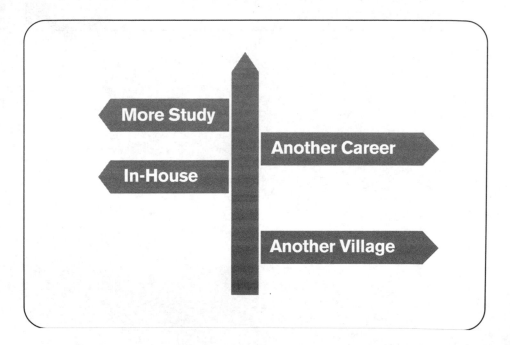

Perhaps your firm has indicated that it will not be keeping on any trainees or not any in your preferred department or perhaps your firm does not have a separate department dealing with the area of law that interests you. Perhaps you really want to live in another part of the country. Perhaps you have decided that the law is after all not for you and your time as a trainee was simply an experiment that did not quite work out.

Even if you know that your firm is in your preferred location and will offer you a position in your preferred area of law, remember that it is at best lazy, and at worst very foolish, just to accept their offer with a sigh of relief. You need to be sure that you are making an informed choice. From the beginning of your training contract you should be practising your observation skills. Whether or not you would want to work in a particular law firm and what your long-term future might be there depends not just on its reputation or the amount that it is willing to pay.

BEFORE YOU COMMIT THERE ARE SOME QUESTIONS YOU MIGHT ASK YOURSELF:

- Is this the only firm where I can do the sort of work that I want?
- Is this where I would get the best work/life balance?
- Why does this department have three partners and no assistants?
- Why are most of the other departments in the firm mentioned in Chambers 500 but this one is not?
- Should I really be willing to work in a department where I do not like the Head of Department?
- Would I get credit for the work that I do, or would my supervisor claim all the credit?
- Do the assistants go to meetings with partners or do the partners keep the clients to themselves?
- How do the partners treat the trainees and assistants in front of other partners or clients?
- What do the other trainees and assistants have to say about the partners I would be working with most of the time?
- Do the assistants in my preferred department get smaller pay rises than assistants in other departments?
- Would it be better to choose another specialism so that I can work without being belittled, because otherwise I like the firm and its ethos?
- Am I already consistently working unreasonably long hours? And would I have to work even longer hours once I qualify?

These questions are directed mainly at ascertaining whether working in your chosen specialism in your present firm is likely to be a happy, productive experience. If you have suspicions that you would not be included in meetings with clients, that your chosen department is less well regarded inside and outside the firm than other departments or that it is less profitable, then you might be better off considering another specialism or looking for another firm entirely.

MORE QUESTIONS

Is staff turnover generally very high or very low compared with other firms, and what could it mean for you? You can get quite a good idea of this by reading the general law weeklies such as the *Gazette*, *The Lawyer* or *Legal Week*, which you can find online or in the firm's library.

How well run is the firm financially? You can get an idea of this by how quickly it sends out its bills after a piece of work is done, by noting how strictly it chases up its clients and by how quickly it pays its own bills. By keeping your eyes and ears open, you can glean a surprising amount of information about this without prying or spying.

How strict is the firm about time-recording? Most lawyers complain about this, but remember that time is money and money is necessary to pay for both your salary and the support services that you enjoy. It may be an office joke that one of the partners has £400,000 of unbilled time, but multiply that among a few of the partners in a large office and suddenly the cash flow does not look so very healthy.

Is the person you are likely to be with after qualification going through a bad patch? Messy divorces take a long time and they have a bad habit of spilling over into the lives of others. When the partner you have been sitting with has just been told by her divorce solicitor that it is likely that she will have to assign half her pension rights to her husband, she is not going to be very happy. If the partner you are sitting with is not divorcing, but is one half of a very unhappy marriage where his wife calls him regularly every morning to berate him about some failing, it is possible, even likely, that his personal ear-bashing will be followed by some fault-finding with your work.

It may seem unfair to base your choice of post-qualification position on someone else's marital problems or unhappiness, but remember that you are not there to be a counsellor for someone else's difficulties or an emotional punchbag for their frustrations. And even if you are

Assess yourself

You might be in a very supportive firm with reasonable partners who do not expect you to sell your soul for your salary, but you still have to be able to perform to the best of your ability and the best of your ability has to be good enough for them. So ask yourself:

- Does it take me longer than anyone else to do this job? If so, why? Is it because I am more meticulous or do I just find It more difficult?
- Do I get taken to meetings? If not, why not?
- How much amending of my work does the partner have to do? Is this correction of English style and punctuation and spelling? Or is it correction of fundamental points of law or procedure? How much effort am I willing to make to get it right?
- When I really try, do I succeed in understanding where I have gone wrong, or is It all still a fog?
- Do I enjoy procedure?
- Do I enjoy drafting?
- Do I enjoy problem solving?
- Do I enjoy reading case law and relating it to legislation?
- Do I enjoy getting documents in order?
- Do I enjoy negotiating in meetings or on the phone?
- Can I put clients at their ease?
- How many people have said that I have done a good job? This could be in the form of a note from a client, a good appraisal report, a casual remark or simply not getting a bawling-out by one of the partners who habitually shouts at his trainees.

Be honest with yourself when you answer these questions. Some of them are directed at which aspects of legal work you actually enjoy and which aspects you abhor.

Others are asking you to assess how you think that you are coping with your training experience and what others think of you. It is unlikely that you will answer all these questions positively. Remember that very few newly qualified solicitors feel totally confident about their new status; in fact many newly qualified solicitors feel that their new status only enables them to know what they don't know. However, answering these questions and thinking about them should give you some idea about what sort of work you enjoy and whether you could and should remain with your present firm.

In a nutshell, does getting up for work in the morning give you a feeling of excitement (at least some of the time) or is it always a drag? Life really is too short to be miserable in your job. Many people will tell you this – others can't because they didn't find out until it was too late.

understanding and helpful, don't assume that they will be grateful. Marital disharmony and additional financial pressure are not conducive to being sympathetic to newly qualified solicitors. And whatever you do, if the partner confides in you or you happen to become aware that things are not exactly rosy at home, never get caught passing that sensitive personal information on to anyone else.

It might help to write down your answers to all these questions, to be sure that you are honest with yourself and not just wallowing in vague emotions. And you need to be even more honest about the questions on the previous page, which are to do with the likelihood of your succeeding in your firm or the area of law that you think that you want to practise. Check out www.rollonfriday.com for comparative salary studies, law firm gossip and insider information.

AN AMICABLE PARTING

If you leave your firm for whatever reason, you will probably be asked to participate in an Exit Interview. This is often billed as an informal chat about your experiences at the firm and what procedures or aspects of training the firm could improve for other trainees or recently qualified solicitors. It is very tempting at this point and in a burst of righteous, 'get it off your chest' triumph, to list all the complaints that you have about anyone and anything, from the quality of the toilet paper to the incompetence of the Word Processing department, the inadequacy of the training, the rudeness of the Head of the Litigation department, the wandering hands of a particular Senior Associate in the Employment department etc.

While this may make you feel better at the time, and the HR person who interviews you may well make agreement noises, remember that the purpose of this interview is twofold. First, it is perhaps to make notes of things that could be improved in the firm – if the HR person is strong enough to put them on paper and then to discuss them with the Managing Partner. Second, it is to make notes about you. At some point in the future the firm will most likely be asked to provide a reference for you. If you have been too trenchantly critical of them, they will be more inclined to gloss over your good points and remember the things that you said about their training and personnel – which in their eyes may appear totally unjustified. It is also not impossible that at some point in the future you will want to return to the village you are now so eager to leave, or even that the new village that you move to will merge with your old one to form a big, new village.

REASONS FOR LEAVING

The safest things to concentrate on in an Exit Interview are the positive reasons for leaving. For example:

■ You want to work in a larger/smaller firm
■ You want to work in a larger/smaller town
■ You are getting married and your future spouse lives in another town
■ Sadly your present firm does not offer sufficient specialisation in the area of law that you would like to concentrate on
■ You have become so interested in Commercial Law that you would like to know more about how business works from the inside and feel that the best way to do this is to go in-house
■ You want to work for the Government Legal Service because you are interested in how Government and the Law relate

Even if you are sure that you never want to see another legal document again in your life and you are going off to work in PR for the Lib Dems or as a rock group roadie, remember that at some point you may still need a reference from the firm that you are leaving. In addition, after a few years in the world of work, you'll see for yourself just how interconnected people networks are. You just never know who you will bump into or even have to work with again in the future. Don't burn bridges if you can help it.

Chapter 21

A NEW LIFE

SPEED READ SUMMARY

- If you are leaving your training firm, make your exit as clean as possible to ensure that you will obtain the best possible reference in the future.

- Before you rush into finding your next job, think about how you would use career coaches, career counsellors and recruitment agents to your best advantage.

- Look again at your personal skills and capabilities and identify the skills and knowledge you gained during your training contract.

MAKING AN EXIT

If you work in a small firm and you are unhappy as a front line solicitor, then the exit road from that firm is probably the only one that is sign-posted. However, if you still find the law interesting and you enjoy other aspects of the working environment in a large legal firm, consider what other roads might be open to you. Increasingly firms fill senior roles in their Marketing and PR departments with qualified lawyers and all PSLs and many librarians also have legal qualifications. Ask yourself whether any of these positions would suit you before you walk away from the career that you have spent at least six years training for.

Use every contact that you have in your firm and in other firms to find out as much as you can about how these people actually spend their days and whether what they do would suit you. And there is an ancillary question.

Whatever your motivations for entering the law, and they can be anywhere on the spectrum between absolutely altruistic to money motivation, you will probably have to accept that it will be unlikely that you will earn as much being a Marketing professional or a PSL as you would staying in actual practice. Ask yourself honestly whether you could be comfortable experiencing the widening difference between your salary in a supporting role and the salaries of your practising colleagues of the same level of qualification.

WHOSE DECISION?

If you are taking the exit road, it will be for one of two reasons. The first is that you have rejected your law firm, and the second is that it has rejected you. Hard as the second alternative may feel, be honest and ask yourself whether this is really a blessing in disguise. Were you really happy there? Was this truly the right role, or even the right career for you?

These days a request that you leave will usually be accompanied by a severance package, which may come not only with money but also with an offer of career coaching with an independent organisation. Law firms take no great satisfaction from getting rid of staff and some are realistic

---

Bad press

Villages which treat their inhabitants badly may be avoided by others in future. One department in one particular City firm had a small, select but fairly vociferous band of critics in other firms who had been treated badly by one of its partners. That did the firm no favours as it struggled to grow that department.

enough to realise that this is their failure as much as yours. (Often it may in fact be more their failure than yours.) They may simply not have generated enough work for someone of your level of qualification. They may have lost some major long-standing clients and are having to slim down or do away with your department altogether. Remember that whatever the circumstances your firm wants a lavender departure, which means:

- The cleanest, most polite, exit process so that your leaving does not tie up unnecessary staff time, either emotionally or physically. If you have been there for some time, and you are popular with your colleagues, your departure will have an effect on the morale of your colleagues – at least for a while.
- The best possible press in the future.

So, however hurt you feel in this circumstance, try to find a friend, preferably someone older and more experienced, who can help you with the process of negotiation towards a settlement. Get the best possible package (one that both sides think is reasonable) – and then move on. Don't skulk away somewhere merely licking your wounds, however hurt you may feel. You can 'nurse your wrath to keep it warm' but that will not pay your bills.

Whatever the reason for your leaving, it is important that you treat this as an opportunity as much as a cause for dejection. Even if you are the one who is choosing to leave, you may still have feelings of failure. Instead think of your departure, anticipated or otherwise, as a chance to re-evaluate your skills and what you want out of life.

PEOPLE WHO CAN HELP

As usual there are many people who can help if you know where to look for them. Don't just look for friends who are willing to listen uncritically to your woes about late nights, unappreciated work and tetchy partners. Your parents, especially if one or other of them has changed jobs frequently or has faced redundancy, may have surprising insights, and, all importantly, may be able to provide you with a roof over your head while you consider your options. Ask what worked for them. Do they have friends that you can talk to?

On a professional level people who can help you fall mainly into three categories: career coaches, career counsellors and recruitment consultants.

Career coaches

If your firm is paying for this, they may already have an arrangement in place with a particular organisation or individual. Don't scorn this just because of the association with your firm, but do try to do some research before you accept them. If you are going to pay for this yourself it's even more important that you try to find out something about the organisation. How long have they been in business? Are they members of any training body? Do you know anyone who has used them?

Most coaches and consultancies will give you a short taster session to see if you 'click'. If you don't have some sort of rapport with a coach you will probably not be willing or able to accept what they can do for you. You should be looking for someone who will lead you to your own realisations about yourself and what your next steps should be, not just someone who will tell you what to do.

Leaving money

If you are asked to leave, this is the time to use the negotiation skills that you have learned over the past two years. Find out what is on offer and also, if possible and discreetly, what other newly qualified solicitors in similar situations in other law firms have obtained. What you should be looking for are good references, possibly outplacement counselling – and certainly money.

You will need money to get you through the process of searching for a new job.

You will most likely be given sufficient to see you through a few months, usually somewhere between three and nine, before you really do have to find another job. Don't be tempted to rush out and buy the expensive suit you have always wanted or to upgrade your car. If you find another job quickly your severance payment will be a useful safety net for the future. If you are not so fortunate you may need to make that money last for longer than you planned, and having a contingency sum set aside will always put you in greater control of your own destiny. If it is your own considered decision to leave, then start saving some bolting money. You will obviously need this if you have decided to get out of the law altogether and either you have a further training course in mind or you really don't know where your future lies. But even if all you are looking for is a job in another law village, start saving, because it's difficult to keep up the same level of commitment in a firm that you have decided to leave, the word may spread that you are looking for somewhere else and your departure may then be swifter than you had anticipated.

Career counsellors

Good career counsellors have amassed a great deal of experience about the sort of character traits that are useful or necessary for all sorts of different careers. There are also many psychometric and personality tests, some of which you may already have experienced as part of the recruitment or training process at your present firm, which may help to suggest what career and what level of responsibility would suit you.

It's a truism, for example, that there are many lawyers whose grasp of detail is not entirely secure but who are wonderful at getting and keeping clients. If you are one of those client charmers, then your need is for strategies to get you into the latter position as quickly as possible. If you are a details sort of person, then you may have to accept that as a legislation lover you will probably never earn as much as the rainmakers, but you could derive just as much satisfaction from a legal career if you can develop strategies for ensuring that you are valued.

However, it is difficult for someone else to point you in the right direction immediately. So treat the analysis sessions as the start of the process and not just the end. Often the character trait analysis is the most useful part of the session rather than the advice that follows. Just because you enjoy working on your own and like the outdoors, does not mean that you have to be a market gardener in the Outer Hebrides; you could equally well be an IP consultant working from home who spends lunchtimes and weekends in the garden.

Recruitment consultants

Even if you are not thinking of changing your job just yet, you should always listen carefully to other lawyers' tales about recruitment consultancies. The level of efficiency and probity does vary enormously, as does their true interest in you. Take a minute to think why this should be so.

Those recruitment consultants who deal with the hiring of young people are usually fairly young themselves. Legal recruitment used to be conducted through agencies whose consultants had not been lawyers themselves; now this is less likely, although it is still unlikely that the consultants will have had many years of actual legal experience. They will be able to tell you about jobs, what level of experience is required, possibly what salary can be expected and will help you to fill out an application form or prepare a CV, but do not expect them to be able to advise you. Even when they do, it would be unwise to rely on this.

Many consultants may be paid on a commission or 'bums on seats' basis. This may lead them to send out as many CVs to as many firms as they can, hoping to make as many hits as possible. You should insist that an agent does not 'spray' your CV around to firms on a speculative basis. Insist that your CV is sent out only to firms that you have agreed may be contacted.

INTERVIEW WITH A RECRUITMENT CONSULTANT

It pays to be well-dressed, polite and uncomplaining about your present village when you go to see a recruitment consultant about a move to a new one. Treat it as yet another practice interview.

Do not give recruitment consultants unnecessary information and do not be bullied into giving information that you do not wish to give which can subsequently be revealed to a potential employer in a casual conversation. One older candidate, who had the good fortune to look younger than she was, refused to give her age to one agency but eventually caved in with a second who promised that it would not reveal it to a potential employer. No interviews arose from the second agency, but there were several through the first and she was hired by a firm which was amused by her age anonymity strategy.

Always remember that initially at least recruitment consultants are not paid by you, but by the firms or companies with whom they either have an ongoing relationship or with whom they want to have one.

You will find that the more senior you get, the more attention you will get from them, as you will now be dealing with headhunters who really want to help you and to build up a long-term relationship with you because you may be in a position one day to instruct them to find candidates for you. As their fee is usually a percentage of the first year's salary of the person they have introduced to a firm, they will earn more by placing a senior rather than a junior lawyer. So, a tip for the future: if recruitment consultants phone you with suggestions about possible moves, always be polite. You never know when you may need them.

SELF-EXAMINATION

But before you see coaches, counsellors or recruitment consultants, and during the search process, you should take a fresh and very close look at your own skills and capabilities. And also at your faults – but don't focus on them for too long.

Ask yourself when, if ever, was the last time that you considered what you really enjoyed and what you had to offer the world of work. The result may surprise you. Some people have never really questioned the assumptions of their parents and immediate family that they would follow in somebody's footsteps or that a particular career was ideal for them. Others, and you could be one of them, have simply found out that their preconceptions about a particular career were wrong and that a few years down the line they are simply disillusioned.

This is the point at which you should challenge yourself as to whether you should be looking for something else. Perhaps you still find the law fascinating, but there are certain aspects of office life that you abhor, or that explaining matters to clients and solving their problems simply does not turn you on. Perhaps you are like the partner who loved to discuss matters legal with his trainee, but the minute that a client came on the phone would signal to his secretary to provide him with a loudly expressed excuse to terminate the conversation.

On the other hand perhaps you enjoy the interaction with people but resent the hours that you may have to spend in your own head working out the solutions to your clients' problems.

Neither of these ways of thinking about legal work is wrong. There are all sorts of opportunities in the law and you may not need to leave the law at all in order to find somewhere where you are comfortable. What you should do is to avoid reaching for the telephone to contact a recruitment consultant in order to order up more of the same. Simply moving to another firm to escape a bossy partner may be all that you need to kick-start your enthusiasm, or perhaps moving later into a marketing or PSL role in your present firm would be a very satisfying move.

It is important to consider all possibilities. You may not have the time or the money to do so again for a long time.

TRANSFERABLE SKILLS

Although we have been urging you up to this point to consider that your training contract is more about employment than training, you will have learned a great deal more than you realise during your time at your firm. You will have acquired what are usually called 'transferable skills'. These range from the simple things that you may have agonised over earlier in your career like simply putting people at their ease to being able to analyse problems quickly and knowing where to go to find the solution.

By this time your firm will have recognised, although you may not have been aware of it, that you have particular strengths which are of use in the office. Sit back and ask yourself what sort of problems and work it is that other people give you to deal with.

Are you the one who:
- is asked to write articles for legal journals?
- is asked to research difficult points of law?
- is asked to give presentations?
- deals with IT?
- gets the office information sources organised?
- is frequently asked to look after clients?

Ask yourself why this is. It could just be that you are exceptionally good at these things. But also ask yourself whether, even if you do them well, you really do enjoy doing them. A woman can be persuaded to buy a dress if she is told often enough that she looks wonderful, but she will not actually wear it if she does not feel comfortable in it.

If you actually do enjoy everything, or nearly everything that you do, but you simply feel unloved and unappreciated, then it's time to pick up the phone to the legal recruitment consultant, vowing that you will be very careful about the next firm that you work for.

If you do not actually enjoy much or any of what you are doing, then you need to do some ruthless analysis of your skills and how they might match up with the requirements for another career. Once you have identified those aspects of your job which you can do and enjoy doing, ask yourself which of your skills can be transferred into another area of work. This is not something to do alone. Ask your friends and family to be brutally honest with you about your strengths and weaknesses, and at the same time try to speak to people who work in any other field in which you are interested.

INTERVIEW FOR ANOTHER FIRM

Interviews that you have at this stage of your career will be different. You will have had at least two years of work experience behind you. If you are interviewing for another legal job, there will be an assumption that you will be totally familiar with office life and your interviewers will have an expectation that you have a reasonable set of technical skills. They are

looking for someone who is more than merely bright and personable.
Before you embark on this type of interview:

■ Research the firm which is interviewing you – thoroughly. Find out what
  deals they have been involved in generally, what cases they have taken
  to court, particularly if they have been successful.

■ Find out as much as possible about the department for which you are
  interviewing. This ranges from details of their work and the type of
  clients they service, to details of the date of qualification and careers of
  the partners and associates in the department. Find out who they have
  been hiring and who they have been 'letting go'

■ Look at the general bias of the firm. If you are a pensions expert, are
  you going to be used merely to sort out the pensions aspects of
  mergers and acquisitions or does the department have a flourishing
  practice of its own? Remember that neither of these is wrong in
  absolute terms, it is just a matter of working out whether there is a
  match for you as well as the firm.

It will also give you some idea of the various technical areas that will be
the focus of your interview. 'Property' is a very wide field, but it has many
subdivisions. To put it at its most basic, if your experience has been in
low-cost residential conveyancing and you want to make the move to a
firm specialising in large-scale commercial development, you will have to
show that you know something about this area already, or that you have
thought about what additional aspects of the law you need to acquire and
also what aspects of your present experience would be of positive
assistance if you were to gain a position with the interviewing firm.

Painting a picture

It will of course be much easier to sell yourself, even if you have been asked to leave, if you are still in employment with your present firm. It is much easier to present yourself as proactive. Even if you are leaving as the result of an acrimonious dispute with your head of department, it is unlikely that you will be given a damning reference unless your behaviour at your present firm has been truly reprehensible. Most firms simply want to resolve sackings and redundancies as cleanly as possible so that they can get back to the legal work at hand. Remember that it is a picture that you are painting, not a black and white photograph that you are submitting in evidence. So you can take a rose-coloured brush to paint the picture of your departure, removing certain inconvenient tufts of grass or broken-down lorries, provided that what you say is actually truthful.

But don't bluff! If you want to move from a corporate tax practice to a private client-focused firm, don't pretend that you know a great deal about trusts and Inheritance Tax if you don't. You will be found out, and some interviewers will take great pleasure in gradually peeling away the layers of your ignorance. Instead, remember that private clients own companies and have VAT issues; it is in these areas that you should be displaying your competence. And it may be precisely because they want to beef up this area of their work that they are interviewing you in the first place.

At the interview you will be asked questions about your present firm. Indeed some interviewers will somewhat unscrupulously use the interview as an opportunity to find out about 'domestic' aspects of your firm. Don't fall into this trap. If you do spill the beans the main thing that they will learn about you is that you are a gossip in a gossipy profession or, more damning, that you can't be trusted to keep a confidence.

The really awkward question

You will certainly be asked why you have left or are thinking of leaving 'such a well-regarded firm'. This is not an opportunity to hatchet the partner that you never want to see again, or inveigh against your firm's obvious bias against ethnic minorities or women. Nor is it the time to say that you have a 'personality clash' with your immediate boss. While your interviewers may appear to proffer sympathy, the unspoken question that will hang in the air is whether you yourself are a difficult person to deal with. If they hire you, will they have to be especially careful that they do not give offence in an unguarded moment? Are you the sort of person who will be looking for unintended insults?

If you have been asked to leave your present firm, you will need to think very carefully about how you present your exit. With a little imagination you can turn something painful into something positive. Note the differences between the following:

'They fired me, because they foolishly thought that my work was not up to scratch.' If you are going to say this, then you may as well not have got up that morning.

'They did not realise my potential, and because I made one tiny mistake they suggested that I leave.' This is not much better. The one thing that partners are constantly concerned about is the possibility of their associates' blunders having an impact on their insurance premiums or, worse, landing them in court.

Positive downtime

Having some time off after a bruising experience can sometimes be surprisingly positive, particularly if you manage your time constructively. Try to look at yourself objectively and assess what might make you even more marketable. If you have identified technical areas that you should know more about, set aside a part of your day to acquire that knowledge.

You may well have more time to keep up-to-date with what is currently happening in your area than if you were doing client work. Try to set aside time to do this by using the library or the internet or, depending on your finances, investing in books or courses. You will make a better initial impression if you look healthy and well-turned out. You may have less money for a while, but you will also have the time to exercise and to spend more time outside. You will not be tempted in the same way to indulge in after-work drinking and eating lazy food.

You will have more time to spend with recruitment consultants, honing your CV and job-specific covering letters, thinking through interview techniques and practising answers to awkward questions. Remember that it takes only one good offer to turn your life around.

'There was not enough work in the department, and I was the one who was asked to leave.' This is a bit better, although it does raise the question as to why it was you and not anyone else who was asked to leave. This may be a good starting point, if you can go on to comment that you were the only associate in a small department where the partners were not able to generate enough work to keep you busy or if the Senior Partner's daughter was preferred to you, but it still leaves the unspoken thought that if you really had been that good, your previous firm would have found some way to keep you on.

'As you may know, there has been a reorganisation in the firm. The partners decided that they would concentrate our Shipping business in the Greek office in the Piraeus, and keep only partners in the London office.' As you are not a partner – yet – this cannot be held against you. It was an operational decision which would have had the same consequence for all the Shipping associates in the London office. Just make sure that it is true before you say it.

'I've learned a lot at my present firm, but I feel that now is the time to move on. There is a great deal of experience in the department, and I have learned a lot about building up relationships with clients and dealing with complex international

Tax structures. However, the department is top heavy so it is difficult to move on to the next stage of taking responsibility. So, I'm looking for a firm that will give me that opportunity. I'm not afraid of hard work.' This is much better, because you have indicated that you have the ability to learn and you have highlighted the twin characteristics that they are most probably looking for: the ability to build up a rapport with clients and technical excellence. And you are prepared to move in order to get what you want.

And an even more awkward question?

If you are not currently employed, it may appear that you have an apparently more difficult task. But that is not necessarily so.

The time spent at a firm whose future you no longer share and where people will no longer be pushing work your way when you are simultaneously trying to find another job, can be very stressful indeed. Simply being out of that office will enable you to relax. However, the immediate stress removal may well produce lethargy and a feeling of uncertainty, which is perfectly understandable because you are distancing yourself from a situation which although stressful you have invested so much to attain.

If you can afford it go for a holiday, however short, get outside, take exercise, keep active, think positively about your future and get rid of the negative feelings about your firm and your experiences there.

When you have placed a little distance between yourself and the firm you have left, you will be in a better position to review what you have actually learned during your training contract and your years post-qualification. To test this, write an experimental covering letter. Sit down with several sheets of paper and jot down lists of the technical expertise you have acquired, of the deals or matters that you have been involved in, the tricky situations that you have helped to resolve and what benefits that experience will bring to a new firm. Consider what you can reasonably say about your former firm with enthusiasm but without breaching client confidentiality.

TAKING A BREAK

Sometimes the reasons that you leave have less to do with the firm than with your present domestic situation or your own personality and how you see yourself in the world. You may, for example, decide to leave your present firm because:

- You want to care for your children or your elderly parents or a sick partner
- You did not have a gap year and have now saved up enough money to spend a year travelling the world
- You want to go back to college to expand your knowledge of archaeology or French or to do an MBA

These are all valid reasons for absenting yourself from the legal world for a while. If and when you want to return to your legal career, think carefully about what you have learned and how your new knowledge can be applied to the benefit of your new employer. And if possible assure them that these experiences will not be repeated any time soon.

RETURNING TO THE PROFESSION

Do not assume that just because you have left the law for a period, you cannot return. The practice of law requires two things above all – legal skills and legal knowledge. If you have acquired the first through your training and post-qualification experience, you will find that determination and hard work will regain the second.

If you have been out of the profession for a short time and simply want to go back to what you know, there are several good (if expensive) courses that will bring you up-to-date in your chosen specialism. If, on the other hand, you are looking for a general refresher course, perhaps to help you to decide whether you want to change specialism, then the Association of Women Solicitors runs a well-established week-long course in Cambridge every September. This is open to male as well as female solicitors, is subsidised by the Law Society and covers the latest developments in black letter law and the latest rules on money-laundering and conduct as well as providing sessions on soft skills. It will also give you a chance to network with other returning solicitors and with practising members of the legal profession who provide the tuition.

JARGON BUSTER

Assistant	An assistant is a fully qualified solicitor who is not a partner.
Associate	An associate is also a solicitor who is not a partner. Some firms call all their assistants associates and some do not use the term at all. Generally it is used for someone who has been qualified for some time. But just to add to the confusion some firms call people associates when they may be made up to partner level, and others call them associates when they have no intention of making them up. It's a good idea to find out what is the policy in your firm, and finding out the policy in other firms that you have dealings with will save you from making silly social errors.
Billing targets	See Chapter 9. They are important. Take them seriously. Typically they range from 1,300 (relatively low) to 2,500 (arguably inhuman).
BVC	Bar Vocational Course. One-year full-time or two-year part-time qualification the Bar Standards Board requires intending barristers to take before pupillage.
Client care letters	These are letters sent to clients which set out the rules of engagement. The Law Society requires that solicitors should send them to clients setting out the terms and conditions of the relationship, which fee-earners are to be working for the client, the rates that they are to be charged out at and what the client should do if he wants to complain. Clients should be asked to sign and return a copy of the letter to indicate acceptance of the terms.
Cost centre	This is exactly what it says. It is a part of the firm or a set of the firm's activities which no one expects to make a profit in itself, although it is possible that on odd occasions these

departments may generate some income and thus reduce their cost to the firm. This covers the Library, the Marketing department, the HR department, the IT department and all other back-up departments. It also for the most part covers PSLs, which partly explains why there can sometimes be animosity between fee-earners and PSLs.

Counsel   Is another name for a qualified barrister. And just to confuse you, it is used by at least one major firm to indicate outstanding solicitors of the same level of qualification as partners who are not in fact partners. The term 'Senior Counsel' is sometimes used.

CPD   This is an abbreviation for Continuing Professional Development. The Solicitors Regulation Authority (SRA) requires that all solicitors, even the most senior, perform at least 16 hours of educational activity per annum as a condition of being issued with their Practising Certificates. So, don't think that qualification will bring an end to your formal legal education – it's just the beginning.

Many solicitors and their firms see the CPD requirement as onerous and unnecessary. They therefore frequently find themselves in the situation, particularly as the annual CPD deadline approaches, of having to attend courses in subjects which are not particularly germane to their practice areas just to get the accredited hours. Take control if you can! When you are qualified think about your own CPD requirement in advance, and try to plan your training a year ahead. This can be an opportunity to make yourself an expert in an area in which you have an interest, and to make yourself more useful to the firm, as you can earn CPD hours for delivering seminars as well as attending them.

Fee-earners   This means simply those who earn fees. There may be people in your firm who are in fact solicitors or barristers of some years' qualification, such as PSLs, Librarians or even Finance staff, but they will not be 'fee-earners' because their work does not directly generate fees. Don't assume however that just because your work generates fees, you are more important than they are.

Human capital	This is what you and all the other employees of the firm are. By employing you, the firm is investing in you and wants to see a return on its investment.
Human Resources	Formerly called Personnel, this department is responsible among other things for implementing decisions concerning the disciplining and hiring and firing of employees.
The Law Society	This is the representative body for solicitors in England and Wales. (See also SRA and Junior Lawyers Division in **Useful Links.**)
LPC	Legal Practice Course. A one-year full-time or two-year part-time qualification that the SRA requires potential solicitors to take prior to commencing a training contract.
Magic Circle firms	Those London firms which consistently deliver the highest profits per equity partner and are involved in the biggest deals. They are traditionally regarded as Allen & Overy, Clifford Chance, Freshfields Bruckhaus Deringer, Linklaters and Slaughter and May.
Managing Associate	This is a term used by some major firms, such as Allen & Overy and Linklaters, to identify associates of four to six years PQE who have a real potential to become partners.
Managing Partner	It is easy to confuse the title Managing Partner with the title Senior Partner. The distinction is similar to that between the Chief Executive (Managing Partner) and Chairman (Senior Partner) of a company. The Managing Partner is responsible for the day-to-day running of the firm in conjunction with the firm's most senior HR, Marketing and Finance professionals. The Senior Partner on the other hand acts as the chairman of the partnership and represents the firm in its dealings with the outside world. This is a very simplistic description and will vary from firm to firm but it is a reasonable place to start when you are trying to work out what happens in your firm. Remember that the balance of power between these two will not be the same in all firms and will very much depend on their budget, the force of their personalities and how they are respected both in and outside their firms.

Matter	This word is used to describe a particular task that you are doing for a client, whether it be buying a house or advising on a competition issue. Solicitors speak about having 'ten new matters' or 'three exciting matters with BloggCo'.
Newly qualified	What you will become once you have completed your training contract and been admitted as a solicitor.
PQE	This is an abbreviation for Post-Qualification Experience. This refers to the number of years since a solicitor has qualified and is a term that has been most frequently encountered in job advertisements. It has been argued that under the age discrimination legislation reference to number of years PQE should not be permitted in job advertisements.
PR	This is an abbreviation for Public Relations and at its most basic you are engaged in this from the first day that you step over the threshold of your firm simply by behaving in an appropriate (or inappropriate!) way. Many firms either maintain a PR function, or more likely retain someone to do their PR for them. If you are asked to assist in this in any way, don't be standoffish on the grounds that this is not legal work. You will be promoting the firm, helping to keep old clients happy and perhaps helping to get new clients. This is in fact what many of the most senior partners do all the time.
Precedent	A precedent is essentially something which has been done before. Many firms have developed their own set of documents which can act as a starting point when you are asked to prepare something for a client, whether it is a will, a lease or a loan note. These will have been drafted and finalised by the more competent solicitors in the firm and may also have been settled by counsel. If you are fortunate they may also come accompanied with drafting instructions. You should always use the firm's precedents and not go off on a frolic of your own. If there are drafting instructions, then pay attention to them, and if you have time look up any legislation and cases referred to. Treat using precedents as a wider learning opportunity if you can.
	Smaller firms may have very few precedents of their own, but the library should contain books of precedents to help you, so before you rush headlong into a piece of tricky drafting, find

out what is available and ask other fee-earners what it is that they use.

Profit centre	This is any fee-earning department of the firm. These exist to make money for the firm, and any department or group which turns from a profit centre into a cost centre is likely to be axed, unless the firm as a whole has decided that that department will operate as a 'loss-leader' back-up to other departments within the firm. For many years firms in the City carried Private Client departments even though there was a perception that they did not make money, because they provided a service to senior executives of the firms' corporate clients and because they nurtured trust and tax expertise which was useful in other departments.
QC	This is an abbreviation for Queen's Counsel. QCs are leading counsel. QC status means that they have acquired a badge of approval conferred on successful barristers by the Lord Chancellor, which effectively enables them to charge higher fees. QCs are also called 'Silks' and those who are promoted to QC status are said to 'take Silk'. QCs charge higher fees than when they were 'Junior Counsel' (i.e. any practising barristers who are not QCs) and usually take on more complex or serious cases. A few solicitors are also QCs.
Senior Partner	See Managing Partner above.
Silver Circle firms	Certain firms which are not as large or quite as profitable as the Magic Circle firms, but are still major players on the London legal scene, are known as Silver Circle firms. Among these are Ashurst, Herbert Smith, Macfarlanes, Mayer Brown, SJ Berwin and Travers Smith.
SRA	The Solicitors Regulation Authority (SRA) regulates the training and conduct of solicitors in England and Wales. During your training contract you will be regulated by the SRA while other organisations associated with the Law Society, such as the Junior Lawyers Division and the AWS, as well as other more targeted groups, can provide you with social activities and representation. (See **Useful Links.**)

USEFUL LINKS

Helpful organisations

Professional

Association of Muslim Lawyers	www.aml.org.uk
Association of Women Barristers	www.womenbarristers.co.uk
Association of Women Solicitors	www.womensolicitors.org.uk They run a Mentoring Scheme, a Maternity Helpline and a Returner Course.
Black Solicitors Network	www.blacksolicitorsnetwork.co.uk
Group for Solicitors with Disabilities	Their website at www.gsdnet.org.uk gives some advice about applying for a position if you have a disability. They may also be able to put you in touch with a mentor.
Junior Lawyers Division	www.lawsociety.org.uk/juniorlawyers Membership of this organisation is available to students with enrolled student status of the Solicitors Regulation Authority, including those working as paralegals, to trainee solicitors and to solicitors who have been practising for up to five years.
The Law Society	www.lawsociety.org.uk

Pastoral Care Portal	This is a general helpline run by the Law Society to assist solicitors and trainees by putting them in touch with the appropriate organisation if they find themselves in difficulties or need advice. They can be reached on 020 7320 5795.
Society of Asian Lawyers	www.societyofasianlawyers.com
Solicitors Regulation Authority (SRA)	www.sra.org.uk

General

All Addictions Anonymous	alladdictionsanonymous.com
Benzact	Advice on addiction to benzodiazepine. www.benzact.org and also www.benzo.org.uk
Council for Information on Tranquillisers and Antidepressants (CITA)	www.citawithdrawal.org.uk
Equality and Human Rights Commission	www.equalityhumanrights.com
LawCare	Helps lawyers and their families to deal with health problems such as depression and addiction. www.lawcare.org.uk
LawCare for Barristers	0800 018 4299
LawCare in Scotland	0800 279 6869
Stonewall	Works to achieve social justice for lesbians, gay men and bisexual people. www.stonewall.org.uk
Talk to Frank	Information and advice about drug abuse. www.talktofrank.com

USEFUL BOOKS

Adler, Mark, *Clarity for Lawyers: Effective Legal Writing* (The Law Society, 2006)

Byrne, Rhonda, *The Secret* (Simon & Schuster, 2006)

Carnegie, Dale, *How to Win Friends and Influence People* (Vermilion, 2007)

Covey, Stephen R., *The 7 Habits of Highly Effective People: Powerful Lessons in Personal Change* (Free Press, 2004)

Cruickshank, Elizabeth, ed.,*Women in the Law: Strategic Career Management* (The Law Society, 2003)

Fisher, Roger and Ury, William, *Getting to Yes: Negotiating Agreement Without Giving In,* ed. Bruce Patton (Penguin Putnam Inc., 2008)

Kennedy, Gavin, *Everything is Negotiable: How to Get the Best Deal Every Time* (Random House Business Books, 2008)

Slapper, Gary, *How the Law Works: A Friendly Guide to the Legal System* (Collins, 2007)

Stoakes, Chris, *All You Need to Know about Commercial Awareness* (Longtail, 2007)

Stoakes, Chris, *All You Need to Know about the City* (Longtail, 2008)

Yate, Martin John, *Great Answers to Tough Interview Questions* (Kogan Page, 2008)

INDEX

ACKNOWLEDGMENTS

Books don't get written without help from other people. In the case of this book so many people have helped us that a detailed list of acknowledgments would provide an object lesson in networking.

The book's genesis was a series of casual conversations with young solicitors, several of whom told us individually of the real culture shock they had experienced when they moved from the academic to the practical part of their training as solicitors. It quickly became a topic that we raised with anyone and everyone that we had professional dealings with, and we soon found that almost everyone we spoke to in the profession had views about how trainees could be better prepared.

Our first acknowledgment must therefore be of the assistance given to us by the many trainees, newly qualified solicitors, professional support lawyers, training managers and law firm partners who have read and commented on this book from its embryonic to its final form. We thank you not only for your helpful suggestions but also for trusting us with the examples from your own experience on which we based much of what is between these covers.

Collaborating on this book has been enlightening and a great deal of fun, but its production would not have been possible without our publisher, James Piesse, who saw the book's potential and demonstrated how streamlined and swift the whole publishing process could be. In addition we should like to express our gratitude to Chris Stoakes and Denis Reed for introducing us to Longtail and to the City Law School and the City University for their practical help and support.

And finally our thanks must go to our friends and families for their encouragement and forbearance during the writing process.